INCARNATIONAL MISSION

Incarnational Mission

Being with the World

Samuel Wells

CANTERBURY
PRESS

First published in 2018 by the Canterbury Press Norwich
Editorial office
3rd Floor, Invicta House
108–114 Golden Lane
London EC1Y 0TG, UK
www.canterburypress.co.uk

Canterbury Press is an imprint of Hymns Ancient & Modern Ltd
(a registered charity)

Hymns Ancient & Modern® is a registered trademark of
Hymns Ancient & Modern Ltd
13A Hellesdon Park Road, Norwich,
Norfolk NR6 5DR, UK

Published in the United States in 2018 by Wm. B. Eerdmans Publishing Co.

Unless otherwise noted, Scripture quotations are from the New Revised Standard
Version of the Bible, copyright © 1989 by the Division of Christian Education of the
National Council of the Churches of Christ in the U.S.A., and used by permission.

British Library Cataloguing in Publication data

A catalogue record for this book is available
from the British Library

978 1 78622 036 3

Printed and bound in Great Britain by
CPI Group (UK) Ltd

For Graeme and Sue

Contents

Preface

This is a book about three things: mission, the world, and being with. I want to thank those with whom I have shared in mission and the conversations that have yielded the reflections that follow.

Thus an invitation from David Warbrick gave rise to chapter 1, debates with Rebekah Eklund and discoveries with Andrew Earis started me on chapter 2, teaching a course on apologetics with Stanley Hauerwas inspired chapter 3, an invitation from Trygve Johnson brought about chapter 4, the witness of Pete Portal and Andrew Grinnell underscores chapter 5, discernment with Keith Daniel and Abby Kocher and dialogue with Robert Pfeiffer triggered chapter 6, countless meetings with Ally Hargreaves underscore chapter 7, many conversations with Greg Jones and Ellen Davis and shared vision with Jo Wells are reflected in chapter 8, the challenge of Hannah Reed and the collegiality of Russell Rook stimulated chapter 9, and the ministry of Richard Carter lies deep in chapter 10. I am blessed to have and to have had such companions in mission.

Christians are prone to using the term "the world" somewhat loosely, setting it alongside the rather rambunctious "flesh" and the very sinister "devil." I have tried here to offer ten dimensions of "world" that view it more hopefully. So many friends, colleagues, and strangers have shown me the kingdom without themselves owning the name Christian. They humble and enrich me.

When I think of those who have been with me in discipleship, ministry, and mission, I cherish those who have loved me and made me want to be as faithful as the person they believed me to be. Among them a precious place goes to Graeme and Sue Walker: companions, disciples, missionaries; to whom this book is a token of thanks.

Not of This Fold

Did you hear the one about the sweet old lady who got onto a train? She found a seat and settled herself down. At the next stop a young man in a business suit swaggered onto the train and sat opposite her. The old lady got out a Bible and started to read and meditate on its words. The young man was curious to find he'd sat next to someone who wasn't preoccupied with a small electrical device, so he maneuvered his line of sight to find out what she was reading. Realizing it was a Bible, he asked, incredulously, "Do you really believe those stories?" The old lady, without moving her head from her book, peered over her half-rimmed spectacles and said, "I most certainly do, young man." Undeterred, the man continued. "What about that old geezer who got swallowed by a fish? How could someone survive in a fish for three days?" "You're talking about the prophet Jonah, young man. I have no idea how that happened, but I look forward to asking Jonah about it when we meet in heaven one day." The young man thought he'd cornered her this time. "Fair enough, but

---

A sermon preached at Duke University Chapel, North Carolina, on April 29, 2012.

what if Jonah's not in heaven? What if Jonah went to hell?" "Well then," replied the old lady, smiling sweetly, "you'll be able to ask him yourself, won't you?"

Think for a moment about what makes this story funny. The old lady represents the way a lot of Christians feel about the church. Old, charming, behind the times, and ineffectual. But it turns out the old lady is full of surprises. Unlike many Christians, she has an uncomplicated faith in the authority of scripture. She also sees no reason to question the ultimate destiny of believers in heaven and unbelievers in hell. More than that, she has no hesitation in talking even to hostile and mocking strangers about her convictions. The young man represents the modern world—young, pushy, impatient, and businesslike, with little use for historic Christianity, seeing the church as a figure of fun. The story's funny because we assume the old lady's weakness, and yet we see the way her simple faith in the eternal power of God exposes the bombast of the young man. If the roles were reversed, and the arrogant young businessman was full of assurance about the old lady's destiny in the fires of hell, the story wouldn't be funny. Quite the opposite, in fact: it would feel like the powerful man was harassing the vulnerable lady with threats and scaremongering.

Bear that in mind as we think about Peter's words to the rulers, elders, high priests, and scribes assembled in Jerusalem, weeks after Jesus's resurrection and ascension. Speaking of Jesus, Peter claims, "There is salvation in no one else, for there is no other name under heaven given among mortals by which we must be saved." What makes Peter's statement so remarkable is that just a few weeks before his speech there was no such thing as Christianity. There was just Jesus of Nazareth and a rag-tag bunch of faltering followers. Jesus died a humiliating, agonizing, and shameful death; and it looked like another dreamer had simply come to a tragic end. But then came Jesus's resurrection, then came his ascension, then came the coming of the Holy Spirit, and in no time here we are, only four chapters into the Acts of the Apostles, and already Peter's making global, universal, eternal claims for the significance of Jesus. When Peter, the spokesperson for an obscure movement of retired fishermen and former tax collectors, says "There is salvation in no one else," then he's either so ridiculous he's funny, or he's so astonishing he takes your breath away.

The point is, those words sound very different coming from a person who's making a courageous statement from a place of social nonconformity and speaking at the risk of death than they do from a place of wealth and security in a country like ours today. To go back to the conversation about Jonah on the train, Peter has all the subversive relish of the old lady; but a contemporary Christian voice saying the same words sounds like the bullying, swaggering, young businessman.

When Christians today get into the kind of conversation the old lady had on the train, the chatter tends to go in one of two directions. In option one, everything gets very dogmatic, and the lines are absolutely clear who's saved and who isn't, and the Jesus who died for our sins turns into a monster who seems content to send a great many people to hell. This Jesus seems so unattractive that it's not at all clear why anyone would ever want to consider spending eternity with him. In option two, everything becomes terribly vague, and the only thing we seem to know for certain about heaven is that everyone gets there. Eternity becomes all terribly democratic and inclusive and starts to sound more and more like a mirror image of contemporary society, and the mystery is why Jesus went to all the trouble of becoming incarnate and dying an agonizing death just to tell us a bunch of things we already know and to save us from a hell that apparently never existed in the first place.

(Just in passing let me wonder why anyone is surprised that church attendance is in decline. If half the church is presenting a faith that makes God out to be a vindictive judge and the other half is making God out to be an anodyne version of themselves, it's actually amazing that anyone goes to church at all.)

So what's the mistake both halves of the church are making? The mistake concerns salvation. The tendency in a democratic society is to get into a constant battle between liberty and equality. This debate has been going on so long and so animatedly that most of us can slip into it as if we were resuming parts in a play we still remember performing at high school. This is how it goes. We hear the unambiguous words, "There is salvation in no one else," and we instantly react out of a commitment to liberty or a commitment to equality.

If we take the first course and react out of liberty, we see that life is made up of laws, some natural, some conventional, and we have more or less complete freedom whether or not to keep those laws; but keeping or not keeping those laws has consequences, and it's no business of anyone else, even God, to protect us from those consequences, because that would be an infringement of our liberty. Thus when Peter says, "There is salvation in no one else," he's uttering a law, if not of earth, then at least of heaven. If we keep that law and follow Jesus, we find salvation; if we don't keep that law, we miss out on salvation. Simple as that. Ignorance of the law is no excuse. That's the attractive elegance of the view expressed by the old lady on the train.

If, by contrast, we react out of equality, we can't countenance the idea that some might get the candy of salvation and some may not. Inequality may have some purpose or unavoidability in the short term, but when it's painted on an eternal canvas it's utterly unconscionable. From this perspective the case of the person who's never heard the name

Christ, or who's been so exposed to the failures and vices of the church that they can't possibly see the wood of Jesus for the trees of his flawed followers, becomes the cause célèbre. It seems wholly unjust, indeed absurd, to deny salvation to someone simply on the grounds of bad luck. Those committed to equality can find it terribly difficult to make any value judgments at all, and it's quite common to hear ardent proponents of equality maintaining that all religions are of equal worth and equal truth, and even that all religions deep down are saying the same thing. Such views are unsustainable once you've got any kind of detailed knowledge of the diversity of the world faiths, which in many cases flatly contradict one another; but many people nonetheless proclaim them passionately out of an unwavering conviction that there's nothing good to be said about salvation unless everyone has it.

What happens is that salvation gets gobbled up in an ongoing argument between freedom and equality. The debate very quickly ceases to be about the nature and purposes of God and instead becomes yet another familiar battle about the source, protection, and distribution of human goods— the kind of debate that dominates our political lives. It's a bit like walking in on a domestic or sibling argument and knowing that anything you say will simply become ammunition in a relentless and interminable quarrel that's got nothing to do with you.

So how can we think more helpfully about salvation? I suggest by turning to the words of Jesus that we find in John chapter 10. "I am the good shepherd. I know my own and my own know me, just as the Father knows me and I know the Father. And I lay down my life for the sheep. I have other sheep that do not belong to this fold. I must bring them also, and they will listen to my voice. So there will be one flock, one shepherd." This tells us more or less all we need to know about salvation. Let's look at it carefully.

5

Here in John chapter 10 we discover what and who we are. We're sheep. We're not rational, independent individuals; we're not entitled to anything, least of all salvation. We're all alike in two respects only. We're all equally lost; and we're all equally loved. We're equally lost in that there's no hope for us outside the sheepfold; and we're equally loved in that the shepherd knows each one of us by name. That's a lot of names: that's a lot of love.

And here we discover what and who Jesus is. Jesus is our shepherd. Jesus has no identity other than to be the one whose greatest concern is our welfare. Jesus seeks in all ways to give us abundant life and bring us into the safety of his sheepfold. He has not the remotest desire for any harm to come our way. And when harm does come our way, what does he do? He lays down his life for us. This isn't some distant, arbitrary deity orchestrating our eternal destiny by push-button remote control: Jesus says, "I lay down my life for the sheep." He isn't some lofty upholder of individual liberty who lets us walk into danger and leaves us alone to face the consequences. Listen to those most wonderful words you ever heard: "I lay down my life for the sheep." There's no length to which Jesus will not go to bring every sheep into the eternal safety of the sheepfold.

But neither does Jesus pretend that there's some kind of flat equality that makes no one sheep any different from any other. He's quite straightforward about it. He says, "I have other sheep that do not belong to this fold." No idealistic equalization of all religions, no pretending that there's such a thing as anonymous Christianity or that people can be regarded as Christians if they pursue other faiths or agnosticism with good will. Jesus calls it exactly what it is. There are sheep who do not belong to his fold. Don't pretend they do. They don't. They may of course not have heard the invitation. But they may well have heard the invitation and turned it down. They may of course have heard it in such a way that made the sheepfold seem very unattractive. But they may well have had every access to the wonder of what this invitation could be and still turned it down.

We're getting to the crucial part. As to those other sheep, that don't belong to this fold, whether by circumstantial accident or by their own conscious design, Jesus says this: "I must bring them also." There's no ambiguity here: it's clearly central to Jesus's mission, part of his identity. He must bring them. He must. It's not about coercing them against their will. If you've ever hung around sheep you'll know that coercing one against its will isn't really an option, even if it weren't already contrary to the good shepherd's heart. But it's absolutely clear that Jesus's mission is not complete until those other sheep find their way to the fold. Salvation isn't something Jesus tosses our way with a shrug of the shoulders as if to say, "Take it or leave it." Salvation is what the good shepherd lays down his life to make possible and continues to offer everyone, every day, in every way, however little we may value or understand it. Salvation, in the end, isn't something God does for our sake and decides on occasion not to waste on the unworthy: salvation is something God does for God's own sake because God has decided never to rest until we dwell in the heart of the Trinity forever.

Note that this is the moment that Jesus changes tense. He says, "They will listen to my voice." Jesus shifts from his earthly purpose in the present tense to its heavenly fulfillment in the future tense. When the veil is pulled away, when ignorance and misunderstanding and accident of history are removed, all sheep will hear Jesus's voice. Think of what happens in the Easter garden to Mary when Jesus calls her by name. Everything falls into place. That's what Jesus is saying will happen to all sheep when they hear his heavenly voice. And then comes the final future statement: Jesus says, "There will be one flock, one shepherd." That's the joy of God's desiring. That's the longing of the heavenly heart. That's the eternal destiny of all sheep: to be one flock, under one shepherd.

I said earlier it's sometimes hard to understand why anyone goes to church at all. I hope now it's clear. Not to ensure our salvation's in the bag; but to realize we're wayward, stubborn, foolish sheep, to be known by name by the shepherd and be drawn toward the sheepfold, to remember the sheep that are not of this fold, and to long for them to be gathered too. Most of all, we come to church to hear the shepherd's voice and discover what it might mean to be one flock.

Because we shall only discover the final unity of freedom and equality, and the meaning of salvation, and the way to share one sheepfold, when we recall this central truth: we all have the same shepherd.

The Mission of Being With

I believe with is the most important word in the Christian faith. This book describes what this conviction means for mission.[1] It's designed to be read alongside its companion volume, *Incarnational Ministry: Being with the Church*, whose structure it replicates but whose context it alters; but it's also written so that it may stand alone. The consequence of those twin aims is that around half of this introduction either closely resembles or repeats what can be found in the introduction to that book.

In this volume I attempt to do three things; this introduction traces what those three things are and how the book weaves them together. The first thing is to explore the notion of being with, already extensively discussed in my three books *Living without Enemies*, *A Nazareth Manifesto*, and *Incarnational Ministry* but about which it turns out I have a few more things to say.[2] In that sense my purpose is further pondering and

1. I should say at the outset it's not my practice to highlight the words with and for with italics or quotation marks—this takes a bit of getting used to but before very long becomes straightforward.

2. Samuel Wells and Marcia A. Owen, *Living without Enemies: Being Present in the Midst of Violence* (Downers Grove: IVP, 2011); Samuel Wells,

probing of an emerging theme in theology. The second thing is to set out some convictions about Christian mission that might stimulate and inspire a person entering, or considering what it might mean to take up, a particular kind or sphere of mission. Thus this is a book designed to stimulate renewal of reflective practice in mission, including but not limited to mission that forms an aspect of ordained ministry. The third is to ponder more deeply what constitutes the mission of being with, as distinct from, and perhaps complementary to, more familiar and established portrayals of mission. Thus I hope to offer some descriptions and distinctions of abiding value in understanding what mission means. These three respective purposes shape the three parts of this introduction.

Being With

In *Living without Enemies* and *A Nazareth Manifesto* I explore four models of social engagement: working for, working with, being with, and being for. Here I offer a brief summary.

Working for is where I do things and they make your life better. I do them because thereby I'm financially rewarded, I receive public esteem, I enjoy exercising my skills, I delight to alleviate your need or hardship, I seek your good opinion and gratitude; perhaps all of the above. Working for is the established model of social engagement. It takes for granted that the way to address disadvantage or distress is for those with skills, knowledge, energy, and resources to introduce those capacities to enhance the situation of those who are struggling. It assumes that the advantaged have abundance,

---

A *Nazareth Manifesto: Being with God* (Oxford: Wiley-Blackwell, 2015); and Samuel Wells, *Incarnational Ministry: Being with the Church* (Grand Rapids: Eerdmans; Norwich: Canterbury, 2017).

which defines them, and that they should maximize that surplus through education and training and exercise it through applying their skills as broadly as appropriate. By contrast, the "needy" are defined by their deficit; if they have capacities, these are seldom noticed or harnessed. Working for identifies problems and focuses down on the ones it has the skills and interest to fix. It then moves on to address further such problems, of which the world is never short. It seldom stops to ask why the recipients of such assiduous corrective measures are invariably so ungrateful.

Working with is a different model. Like working for, it gains its energy from problem-solving, identifying targets, overcoming obstacles, and feeding off the bursts of energy that result. But unlike working for, which assumes the concentration of power in the expert and the highly skilled, it locates power in coalitions of interest, initially collectives of the like-minded and similarly socially located, but eventually partnerships across conventional divides of religion and class around common causes. Its stumbling-blocks are not the maladies that working for identifies; they are pessimism, apathy, timidity, lack of confidence, and discouragement. By the forming of networks and the creation of a movement where all stakeholders come together and it's possible for everyone to win, working with establishes momentum and empowers the dispossessed.

Being with begins by largely rejecting the problem-solution axis that dominates both the previous models. Its main concern is the predicament that has no solution, the scenario that can't be fixed. It sees the vast majority of life, and certainly the most significant moments of life, in these terms: love can't be achieved; death can't be fixed; pregnancy and birth aren't a problem needing a solution. When it comes to social engagement, it believes one can seldom solve people's problems—doing so disempowers them and reinforces their low social standing. Instead, one must accompany them while they find their own methods, answers, approaches— and meanwhile celebrate and enjoy the rest of their identity that's not wrapped up in what you (perhaps ignorantly) judge to be their problem. Like working with, being with starts with people's assets, not their deficits. It seeks never to do for them what they can perfectly well, perhaps with encouragement and support, do for themselves. But most importantly be- ing with seeks to model the goal of all relationships: it sees problem-solving as a means to a perpetually deferred end, and instead tries to live that end—enjoying people for their own sake.

Being for lacks the energy and hopefulness of working with and working for, yet also lacks the crucial with that char- acterizes being with and working with. It's the philosophy that's more concerned with getting the ideas right, using the right language, having the right attitudes, and ensuring products are sustainably sourced, investments are ethically funded, people are described in positive ways, and account- able public action is firmly distinguished from private con- sumer choice. Much of which is good; but in its clamor that Something Must Be Done, it invariably becomes apparent that it's for somebody else to do the doing. The alternative to unwise action becomes not engaged presence but cynical withdrawal: multiple causes are advanced, but their untidy details and complexities are often disdained. Full of criticism for working for and working with, apt to highlight the appar- ent passivity of being with, it lacks a concrete alternative to any of them. And yet in an information-saturated, instantly judging, observer-shaped internet age, it's the default posi- tion of perhaps the majority.

Having characterized these four models and recognized the degree of overlap between them, the next step is to lo- cate them theologically. *Living without Enemies* and *A Nazareth*

Manifesto do this by highlighting the shape of Jesus's life, as the Gospels record it. One can see the Old Testament as a study in perceiving the God who is for us—most obviously creating the world, and delivering Israel from Egypt—in creative tension with the God who is with us, represented most significantly by the covenant at Sinai and the sense emerging during the Exile that in Babylon God was present to Israel in a more profound way than simply delivering the people from crisis. Over and again Israel protests there's no use in God being for us; we want to see some evidence, some action—work for us, at least with us.

This is the context into which Jesus emerges: "O that you would tear open the heavens and come down!" (Isa. 64:1). Jesus is presented in the Gospels as the savior who works for us not by defeating the Romans but by forgiving sins and opening the gates of everlasting life—achievements concentrated in his passion, death, and resurrection but anticipated in earlier healings and miracles. But this is not all Jesus does: he spends perhaps three years, largely in Galilee, calling, forming, and empowering followers, formulating a message for them to share, building alliances, and confronting hostility. One can see the "saving" as working for, focused on a week in Jerusalem; and the "organizing" as working with, spread over those years of public ministry. But that still leaves perhaps 30 years in Nazareth, give or take a spell as a baby in Egypt. And here's the question: if Jesus was all about working for, how come he spent around 90 percent being with (in Nazareth), 9 percent working with (in Galilee)—and only 1 percent working for (in Jerusalem). Are those percentages significant—and do they provide a template for Christian mission? Surely Jesus knew what he was doing in the way he spent his time; or do we know better?

This is the theological foundation upon which, in A *Nazareth Manifesto*, having sought to dismantle the stranglehold working for has on the Christian imagination, I elucidate eight dimensions of what being with actually involves. These are my best attempts to describe how the persons of the Trinity are with each other.

- The first is *presence*, which seems obvious until you realize that neither working for nor being for necessarily requires presence: they can often operate from a safe distance. Presence means being in the same physical space as the person with whom you are engaging.
- Next comes *attention*, which turns generality into particularity and transforms "showing up" into focused interaction. Attention requires one to harness concentration, memory, emotion, intellect, gaze, scrutiny, wonder, and alertness here and nowhere else, directly and without mediation.
- Then there is *mystery*. This rests on distinguishing between a problem—which has a generic quality, can be perceived equally well by anybody, can be addressed from the outside, and can be solved using skills acquired elsewhere—and a mystery, which is unique, can't be fixed or broken down into its constituent parts, is not fully apparent to an outsider, but can only be entered, explored, and appreciated. Treating death, for example, as a problem risks wasting energies pursuing solutions, many of which take one away from a person's presence and divert attention elsewhere—thereby missing the call to be with someone as he or she enters a great mystery.
- Lest all this seem too solemn and earnest, the fourth dimension is *delight*. This is the recognition of abundance where conventional engagement is inclined only to see deficit. Delight rejects the template of how things should be and opens itself to surprise and humor and subversion and playfulness. Delight is glad to take time where conventional engagement is overshadowed by urgency.

- The next two dimensions are in some ways a pair. *Participation* names the way with is indispensable and unsubstitutable. It diverts attention from what is done to ensuring the right balance of who does it. Of the hundred reasons to bypass being with, efficiency is near the top of the list. Participation says there's no justification for leaving someone behind and queries whether our hurry to get somewhere is rooted in our reluctance truly to engage with the person with whom we are traveling.

- By contrast, *partnership* is more prepared to see how respective gifts can, when appropriately harnessed, together enable a team to reach a common goal. Partnership sees how the gifts of the "needy" person, habitually obscured by the working-for impulse to be helpful on one's own terms, can make unique contributions to common projects. In this sense it comes within the territory of working with and indicates how closely working with and being with sometimes resemble one another.

- The dimension that encapsulates and epitomizes all the previous ones is *enjoyment*. This rests on Augustine's distinction between what we use, which runs out, and is a means to some further end, and what we enjoy, which is of value for its own sake, an end in itself. Being with, simply put, is enjoying people whom the world, having no use for, is inclined to discard.

- Finally *glory* names the purpose of all things: the opening words of John's Gospel ("the Word became flesh ... and we have seen his glory," 1:14) demonstrate that the epitome of glory, and the originating purpose and final goal of all things, is God being with us in Christ.

Each of these dimensions is rooted in the life of the Trinity and embodied in the life of Jesus, as chapters 8 and 9 of *A Nazareth Manifesto* describe. My concern there and here is

not to discredit the other three models but to describe vividly
and persuasively what being with actually involves.

Mission

I understand the Christian life to come in three parts: discipleship, ministry, and mission. These refer to how one's faith
shapes the self, the church, and the world, respectively. My
initial reflections on being with, as recorded in *Living without
Enemies* and *A Nazareth Manifesto*, largely concerned mission,
and mission is again the subject of this book. The subject of
the book that accompanies and complements this one, entitled *Incarnational Ministry: Being with the Church*, is discipleship
and ministry.

Discipleship is being with God as shaped by being with
oneself, one's community of faith, one's close relationships,
and the wider creation. Discipleship overlaps with ministry
in several ways. Those engaged in ministry never stop being
disciples. But they need to distinguish between their own
response to God (discipleship) and what's most helpful for
the community as a whole (ministry). Ministry means taking
up a specific role in order to help build up the church. That
role may be formal or informal. Ordained ministry refers to
the setting-aside of certain people, usually involving extensive formation, education, and training, to carry out fundamental roles in a Christian community, often including the
performance of sacraments, the preaching of the Word, the
leading of worship, and the convening of the body's decision-
making process. But ministry is not wholly, largely, or most
importantly about the activity of the ordained. Ministry is
whatever is done among and within the body of believers
to build up that body or to enable that body to practice its
convictions together.

The third dimension of the Christian life is mission. Whereas ministry seeks to know Christ and make Christ known within the body of believers, mission addresses the world—all that has taken the freedom of God's patience not yet to believe. But mission often describes that world as the kingdom—thus anticipating that it will be the theater of God's epiphanies, the sphere of the Spirit's work beyond the church, where disciples are humbled by acts of charity the church could seldom encompass, surprised by goodwill that puts the church to shame, and challenged by examples of integrity, courage, kindness, and wisdom the church badly needs. The gospel is not something that belongs to the church, and its propagation is not limited to the church's imagination or by the church's shortcomings: the gospel belongs to the Holy Spirit, and the church is as often catching up with it as advancing it, as often humbled to find it already at work wherever missionaries go as it is blessed to bear it into new hearts and homes, as often drawn into mission to find it as to spread it.

The great narrative of the Holy Spirit is the Acts of the Apostles. We could call the Gospels the Acts of Jesus and the book of Acts the Acts of the Holy Spirit. The Holy Spirit makes present the Jesus of the past, born in obscurity and amid hostility, ministering with a close community, a wider circle of the poor, and in the face of antagonism, dying after trial, torture, and agony, rising before many and being taken up to heaven; and the Jesus of the future, who will come again to unite heaven and earth in a new realm of joy and perfect freedom, in an unending relationship with God the Trinity, in which all creation will worship, be God's companions, and share God's banquet. The Holy Spirit makes the Jesus of yesterday and the Jesus of forever present today in regular and surprising ways. The regular ways are those encountered in discipleship and ministry: sacraments, personal and corporate prayer, reading and proclaiming Scripture, and gestures of mercy and kindness. The surprising ways are the territory of mission: the wisdom or kindness of a stranger, the depth of community that emerges in the face of tragedy, the mistakes that turn into God's opportunities.

Mission is about these surprises. One pastor spent some time serving a church in Ghana. It so happened that the church didn't have enough money to put any glass in the windows. This had the advantage that it let a bit of air in. The only problem was that there was also quite a strong breeze, so they found that when they brought papers into the building the papers blew all over the place. Eventually they decided that having the wind blowing through the church was intolerable, so they got together enough money to put glass in all the windows. The result was simple: the wind blew the roof off. The lesson is that you can't dictate how the Holy Spirit will act. The Holy Spirit is to be received, not grasped. It sets its own agenda. Mission is responding to what the Holy Spirit is doing in the world.

The Mission of Being With

This book comes in two broad parts, with a chapter in the middle that has a foot in both camps. The first part considers individuals in relation to their standing before God—not as judged by a third party but as identified by themselves. Leaving out disciples, who are the concern of ministry, I consider what mission means to those who are not disciples. What is vital is to recognize that people who are not disciples are so for a number of reasons, and perceive the church, and God, with a variety of attitudes. Not able to cover that diversity comprehensively, here I consider five kinds of unbeliever in the first five chapters.

The first kind is the lapsed: those who were once disciples, in many cases happily so, and are no longer. My contention here is that a great many, perhaps the majority, of the lapsed are so not because of their own laziness, or more active form of sin, but because of the church's failure—a failure they have been unable or unwilling to countenance or forgive. Thus I start the book in an attitude of humility that the church in mission has often lacked: that people who don't believe are at least as likely to have been rejected by the church as to have done the rejecting themselves. Before looking out at a field ripe for harvest, the church needs to recognize what it has failed to do with what has already been in the barn.

I then move, more encouragingly, to seekers. Being with the lapsed can be a sobering realization of how much the church has let people down and fallen short of what God calls it to be. Being with seekers is more often a refreshing reminder of the wonder of God, an iridescence that's more than capable of shining through the shortcomings of the church. There is a good deal more glory here. It should be that the experience of becoming a disciple should be one of entering, perhaps for the first time, a culture in which one is enjoyed rather than used. If so, being with has borne fruit in both ministry and mission.

The third kind of unbeliever is perhaps the most subtle: those of no professed faith. Here it's important to hold together two things that sit uneasily beside one another: one, that a disciple frequently has no comprehension of how a person can be a happy unbeliever, for such a state seems, to many Christians, both irrational and unbearable; two, that a great many people are exactly that, and experience no "God-shaped hole," and see nothing in the church to attract or intrigue. Being with these twin truths is the heart of this chapter.

Then I explore the most obvious kind of non-disciples: those of other faiths. Here there is a lot of disentangling of inadequate categories and unwise judgments about traditions of faith outside the Christian penumbra. There is also, again, need for a good deal of humility, and of honest acknowledgment of what Christians' motivation is when they are drawn into the company of members of other traditions. Like the other fields, it is a huge subject, but one in which the eight dimensions of being with have a good deal to contribute.

The least subtle kind of unbelievers, at first glance, are the hostile. Here I don't prioritize the person who writes vitriolic condemnation of the church and all its beliefs and works on a blogsite, or even those who make generalized connections between religion and violence and blame Christianity for all the ills of the world—for those are frequently to be numbered among the ranks of the lapsed, their anger a form of hurt and their hostility a retained pursuit of righteousness. Instead I try to establish what resources are needed to be a missionary—or even just a disciple—in adverse circumstances, where those around you wish you harm, and where the Holy Spirit in the form of the gift of the stranger is very hard to discern.

The sixth chapter concerns the neighbor. It's a transition chapter because like the early chapters it concerns individuals, but like the later chapters it's not primarily concerned with the question of faith or unbelief. It is a meditation on the anxiety of being overwhelmed by the needs of others, an anxiety that might make disciples draw back from mission and confine their vision to ministry: but it concludes that being overwhelmed simply comes with the territory of mission or ministry, and that the one who overwhelms us is Jesus. It could also be read as a study in the challenges of engaging with mission as an outworking of discipleship rather than also as an outworking of ministry: for the two key examples are ones in which individuals strive to solve great hardships largely on their own.

In the last four chapters of the book I move from the individual to the corporate, from the question of faith-sharing to a more general notion of witness, from a notion of anyone, anywhere to an assumption of particular context. A group of people gathering together out of common interest is an association. A collection of people, customs, and usually buildings that develops a public identity that transcends time, and is seen by most as constituting a good in itself beyond what goods it produces, is an institution. Everything that fills the gap between the two is an organization. I start by looking at organizations, seeking to break down their mysteries not just to understand them but to make them less alien to the church. This is done so that disciples may not despise or scorn them as somehow godless, inordinately admire them for somehow being more "effective" than churches, or, just as serious, be content to live in two worlds, organization and church, without the two impinging on the other.

I then move in chapter 8 to institutions, a world that generally feels altogether more comfortable to those used to ministry. To do so I relate my own experience of seeking to be with a large institution over several years, how I went about it, what I thought I was doing, and where it met with rewards.

In the next chapter I consider what it means to be with government. This requires wider considerations of politics more generally and the church's relation to the state. But it also involves a sense of the church's own politics and, just as importantly, a congregation's willingness and commitment to foster a politics in its own neighborhood that places the actions of government in proper perspective. While I don't have a chapter on associations, there is plenty of reflection on associational life here. The chapter is a warning for everyone in the church and beyond that if you expect to get more from government than you put in, you have to take responsibility for the results.

Finally I consider the excluded, whom I take to be those who do not hold a strong place in organizations and have not found collective strength in civil society or representation in government to compensate for, address, or rectify their vulnerability and who have been exploited as a result. Again, much of the work at the outset is to clarify and identify different kinds of exclusion, the better to judge what it means to be with people in each context.

The book is not a comprehensive treatment, but it aims to provide breadth in the subjects it covers as well as depth in the methods it proposes. I imagine the reader may miss a treatment of the approaches and aspirations of humanitarian aid in the developing world; this is because such issues were discussed (as perhaps the most obvious clash between working-for and being-with perspectives) in A Nazareth Manifesto. The reader may likewise, in the face of the ecological crisis, search in vain here for a discussion of what it means to be with creation; I have chosen to consider being with creation as an aspect of discipleship, rather than a context of mission, and have thus included it in Incarnational Ministry. This is because I understand being with creation as inextricable from being with oneself and the church as the context for being with God.

Each chapter has more or less the same shape. In every case I discuss the eight dimensions of being with as elaborated in chapter 8 of A Nazareth Manifesto and summarized above. I don't always keep the same order or regard each one in each case as being of equal significance. In many cases I offer an introductory section that explains why I see this theme as vital for mission and breaks the theme down into constituent elements before moving to the eight dimensions of being with. But the intention is to use these dimensions to come to grips with each context, to show just how much vigor they, taken together, offer to even the most troubling circumstances, to test the categories and highlight places where some are, in some cases, less helpful or pertinent, and to amplify each dimension so that by the end one has a richer notion not just of mission, and of being with, but of each of the dimensions themselves.

I start and end, as I did in A *Nazareth Manifesto* and *Incarnational Ministry*, with a sermon. The way I write theology is uncomfortable with conventional distinctions between theology and doxology. Many of my theological ideas appear first in sermon form, and it is in sermons that God's people are significantly shaped for ministry and mission. Thus this study begins in worship and encounter with the Word, steps into a considered project of meditating upon the mission of being with, and finishes with worship and encounter with the Word.

The book is largely a distillation of insights derived from twenty-five years as a disciple, and a member of the church, in mission: what I'm describing is the person I have wanted to be, the ministry I have sought to embody. I'm the first to recognize I'm a poor example of much that I propound; but I believe it's nonetheless worth propounding. Once, when I shared these ideas at a conference, one of the respondents suggested what I was doing was challenging the distinction between missiology and ethics (just as I have long challenged the distinction between theology and ethics, and doubted the designation "practical theology" because I questioned any theology that supposed it was not practical). I like that interpretation. In many ways this book brings together the arguments and reasonings of my three most substantial books, *Improvisation, God's Companions,* and A *Nazareth Manifesto.*[3] The

3. Samuel Wells, *Improvisation: The Drama of Christian Ethics* (Grand Rapids: Brazos; London: SPCK, 2004), especially chapters 10 and 11; and *God's Companions: Reimagining Christian Ethics* (Oxford: Blackwell, 2006), especially chapter 5.

connection with the third is obvious: this book, and its companion *Incarnational Ministry*, together form a kind of sequel. Readers of *God's Companions* may feel similarly—that this is a second book in the same spirit—one that sees God giving everything we need to follow faithfully, and one that roots theology in the practices of the local church. Perhaps less obviously, this book also draws significantly on *Improvisation*—most extensively on the ability to overaccept and reincorporate, central to that book, and at the heart of the mission of being with, as this book shows.

But this book seeks to be something beyond offering worked examples of being with, identifying the particular contexts of mission, and drawing together insights from a career as a pastor and a theologian. It seeks to be a meditation on the ways of God; a prayer of a reflective, joyful practitioner, grateful for the opportunity to meet God in such privileged and sometimes surprising settings. Its sentences can be read quickly, so as to grasp some of the dimensions of what being with implies in various contexts that I assume the reader has encountered or soon will. But each sentence is also written so that it may be read slowly, reflectively, and over again, as a prism reflecting on faith, mission, God, and, in several cases, the transfiguration that can come through and beyond setback and suffering. Whether a book can be at the same time a polemic for a different approach to mission, a guide for its conduct, the advancement and amplification of a promising theological motif, and a meditation inviting devotion and more reflective practice is for the judgment of the reader. It will no doubt be different things to different people. But all of these things dwell in its writing; and in the living that preceded and informed it.

CHAPTER 1

Being with the Lapsed

The key difference between being with the church (incarnational ministry) and being with the world (incarnational mission) is that in the church one can assume that
ministry is recognized and discipleship sought, whereas in
the world one can make neither assumption. This constitutes
a huge difference of approach, understanding, and purpose.
Thus there are some people who have made profound, and
sometimes public, mistakes, or have fallen into damaging or
deceitful patterns of behavior, yet still long to be whole and
look to the church and its representatives to help them "come
to themselves" like the prodigal son. I call them the troubled,
and I consider being with them in *Incarnational Ministry*. By
contrast, others may have made no particular step away
from the church's lifestyle norms and yet have allowed a distance to grow up between themselves and the fellowship of
faith, having in the process lost respect for the authority and
ceased to seek the guidance of the church's representatives. I
call these persons the lapsed, and I consider being with them
to be a form of mission.

Of all the titles Jesus adopts and descriptions Jesus accepts, perhaps the most resonant is that of the good shep-

herd. John 10:1–16 suggests a number of things about Jesus as a good shepherd. He enters by the gate of the sheepfold, in contrast to the thief and the bandit. He calls his own sheep by name and the sheep follow him because they know his voice. He comes so that the sheep may have life and have it abundantly. He lays down his life for the sheep, in contrast to the hired hand, who runs away. He has other sheep that do not belong to this fold whom he must bring also, that they may listen to his voice, so that there will be one flock, one shepherd. This sets out a wide-ranging agenda for incarnational mission. But the image of Jesus as shepherd is associated above all with Luke's parable (15:4–7):

> Which one of you, having a hundred sheep and losing one of them, does not leave the ninety-nine in the wilderness and go after the one that is lost until he finds it? When he has found it, he lays it on his shoulders and rejoices. And when he comes home, he calls together his friends and neighbors, saying to them, "Rejoice with me, for I have found my sheep that was lost." Just so, I tell you, there will be more joy in heaven over one sinner who repents than over ninety-nine righteous persons who need no repentance.

This parable (though it does not actually use the word "shepherd"), together with the resonances of John 10 and Psalm 23, has lodged a fundamental, perhaps definitive image of mission in the church's mind: that of the good shepherd who goes out at considerable risk, in possible neglect of the regular flock, and out of love for the lost sheep, into the wilderness and searches until it is found—and whose greatest joy, above all other joys, is to restore, rehabilitate, and reintegrate the once-lost sheep into the flock, now and forever, in the spirit of the prodigal's father ("this brother of yours was dead and has come to life; he was lost and has been found," Luke 15:32). Hence being with the lapsed starts from **glory**— the glory of the joy in heaven over the restoration of the lost. The vital point about starting with glory is that being with the lapsed is first about recognizing and acting upon the grief and impoverishment of the flock and the angels in heaven over the absence of one irreplaceable sheep—and only secondarily about that lost sheep's isolation and need to be found. It's not a patronizing, judgmental, and self-centered statement that no one can flourish outside the fellowship of faith; it's a humble acknowledgment that the body of Christ is in pain and is not all it could be if a finger is missing.

Thus in drawing together John's and Luke's accounts of Jesus as shepherd we can delineate three strands: (1) ministry to the flock—knowing by name, leading, giving abundant life, laying down his life; (2) mission beyond the flock, seeking sheep "that do not belong to this fold" so that one day there will be one flock, one shepherd; and (3) mission to those who were once of the flock, but who have "like sheep...gone astray;...all turned to [their] own way" (Isa. 53:6) or, in the words of the 1662 Prayer Book, "have wandered and strayed from [God's] ways like lost sheep [and] have followed too much the devices and desires of [their] own hearts." Perhaps the most neglected of these strands is the third; but this third group, those who were once of the flock but have now wandered away—or been left behind, antagonized, or rejected— could be the most revealing of the three.

One pastor went to see a woman of more senior years. She'd grown up in Wales. She'd left the church when she was a young woman. Ah, thought the pastor, this is a familiar story. A young person is raised in the church, but when they become a young adult either it turns out the faith hasn't taken deep root or they decide to get outside and smell a different air for a while. But clearly, now that she was over ninety, she thought it was time to give the church a second chance. Took her time, the pastor thought, but, fair enough, the church has been patiently waiting for you all this while, like the father did for the prodigal son. Curiosity led the pastor to take a slight risk. "May I ask what it was that led to you being away from the church for seventy-five years?" Nothing to lose, the pastor thought; may learn something. But the pastor forgot the first rule of the inquirer: never ask a question to which you might get an answer you're not ready to hear. The pastor was in for a shock; a shock that would leave a lasting effect on a whole ministry.

"It was when we wanted to get married. We were in love. The rector wouldn't marry us." Well, this sounds romantic, the pastor thought, and, always a soft touch for the romantic twist on a story, blundered in where angels fear to tread. "So was there something wrong," the pastor wondered, "was your husband previously married, or were you too young, maybe?" "No," she said calmly, trying hard not to be patronizing or angry. "The rector looked at my hand. You see, I worked in a mill. I had an accident when I was sixteen." She gently, undemonstratively, held up her left hand. The last three fingers were missing. "The minister said that, since I didn't have a finger to put the wedding ring on, he couldn't marry us."

The color drained from the pastor's face, and the pastor reacted with the disbelieving half-laugh one coughs out when one hears something so ridiculous that it just has to be funny, but in fact isn't funny at all but deeply, deeply horrifying. It was so absurd that no one could make it up. It had to be true. Quickly the pastor felt that seventy-five years away from the church was pretty lenient. "And dare I ask what brings you back to the church now?" the pastor said, having learned nothing, but feeling a desperate need to hear her answer. "God's bigger than the church," she replied. "I'll be dead soon. The Lord's Prayer says forgive if you want to be forgiven. So in the end that's what I've decided to do."

"The fault, dear Brutus, is not in our stars / But in our-selves, that we are underlings."[1] When Jesus portrays him-self as the good shepherd, there can be no explanation for a sheep's becoming lost other than the sheep's own misadven-ture, folly, ignorance, or perversity. But when the church sees itself as the good shepherd, it's likely the reality is very differ-ent. The church tends to see the lapsed as those who have thrown away a precious gift out of their own irrationality. But this shows how a too-quick identification of the church with the good shepherd can prevent the church's representa-tives from seeing what the lost sheep represents. That Welsh millworker suggests a different narrative. She hints at a story in which the lapsed are those who await the opportunity to save the church. After seventy-five years, she gives the church another chance. The question is whether the church is ready to seize that chance the second time around.

Whereas with ministry, **presence** is largely unproblem-atic—taken for granted, sought, longed-for, requested—with mission, presence is invariably complex, questioned, awkward, resented; a cause of suspicion, misunderstanding, or discomfort, and certainly something to be negotiated, earned, and cherished. In the case of the lapsed, there may well be a sense of guilt or regret, a change of life circum-stances that might incur shame if subject to exposure, or at least a certain defensiveness and anxiety about being judged or condemned. Few who have left a community anticipate the presence with them of a still-active member of that com-munity as anything other than an occasion for censure or the expression of disappointment. An encounter in the form of ministry is likely to be planned, anticipated, expected; but a conversation in the mode of mission is rather more prone to be accidental, coincidental, spontaneous—in the grocery

1. William Shakespeare, *Julius Caesar*, Act 1, Scene 2.

store, at the car wash, at a ball game: the rules are unclear, the courtesies aren't established, neither the length nor the content of the dialogue are agreed. Presence becomes truly incarnational when it's intentional—when it takes the risk of initiating contact and proposing to meet, or, in the case of a surprise encounter, looking to continue the conversation over coffee (then or later), or of being willing to visit another's territory—a tangible expression that says "I recognize that there's another legitimate, perhaps more significant and likely unheard, point of view."

Presence acknowledges, however subtly, that there is some degree of conflict going on—that there is to some degree pain, disappointment, hurt, or at least bewilderment on one side or both. At a minimum level, one party appears to value membership of the "flock" more highly than another; probing deeper, the "lost sheep" may feel uncomfortable that they have lost the joy in faith they once had, or they may have only recently admitted that the joy was never there to start with; they may feel difficulty on account of the break-up of a relationship or some other kind of falling out; or they may harbor resentment or hurt about mistreatment or a profound failure on the part of the flock or one of its representatives. Being present crosses the threshold of embarrassment, anger, discomfort, sadness, or indifference in a spirit of not reproach but humility, not self-righteousness but gentleness, not defensiveness but kindness. It recognizes there are often a number of strands contributing to why a person becomes numbered among the lapsed—some habit, some circumstance, some reasoned, some emotive—and that it's unlikely a person will quickly or easily articulate the narrative or perhaps fully comprehend it alone.

Moving to this place of greater understanding (for the lapsed themselves as much as for the one imitating the good shepherd by seeking out the lost) is the move from presence to **attention**. What might seem the obvious explanation, but turns out almost never to be the case, is that a person has simply ceased to hold sufficient conviction in the plausibility of Christian claims in the face of contemporary and timeless reasons not to believe. The truth is that being part of a flock has always been at least as much about belonging as believing, and that if one asks people why they don't believe they invariably come out with a list of objections more than familiar to members of a congregation who, while reckoning seriously with such factors, nonetheless don't regard them as decisive. What attention frequently discloses is that the one thing that turns lingering doubt and abiding skepticism into withdrawal and sometimes hostility is not philosophical misgivings but moral exasperation.

Dominic Erdozain makes the same point with lucid attention to historical detail and biography.[2] He attacks the complacency of Christians, both lay and scholarly, in failing to realize how often the responsibility for rebellion against the faith lies squarely at their own door. (He is equally keen to combat the pervasive secular compulsion "to build a narrative of objective, scientific reason triumphing over ignorance and superstition" [262].) Erdozain quotes these sobering words of Ludwig Feuerbach: "Faith gives a man a peculiar sense of his own dignity and importance. The believer finds himself distinguished above other men, exalted above the natural man; he knows himself to be a person of distinction, in the possession of peculiar privileges; believers are aristocrats, unbelievers plebeians. God is this distinction between and pre-eminence of believers above unbelievers, personified" (237). What Feuerbach perceives is the way Christianity

2. Dominic Erdozain, *The Soul of Doubt: The Religious Roots of Unbelief from Luther to Marx* (Oxford: Oxford University Press, 2016). Hereafter, page references to this work will be given in parentheses in the text.

has too frequently become a pretext for arrogance—a cover for complacency: Feuerbach, in an insight horrifying to Christians but nonetheless one of their own making, sees faith and love at war and reacts by asserting a pure, atheist virtue of love in the face of the ghastly legacy of faith. The point is not to accept Feuerbach's reduction of God to a projection of believers' own need for social superiority: it's soberly to admit how much evidence he has for his accusation.

Close attention to the heart-searchings of the lapsed reveals to the missionary numerous examples of people, perhaps not so philosophically sophisticated, but in many other respects just like Feuerbach: earnest and upright citizens, drawn to the God of Jesus Christ, but inclined to see Christianity's precision and haste to judge as part of the evil that integrity must resist. Erdozain charts how the church has repeatedly become a factory of fear, offering little besides doom, destruction, and selective redemption. Unbelief came to be fueled, in the words of George Eliot, by fear of "a God who instead of sharing and aiding our human sympathies, is directly in collision with them." Eliot's unbelief, like that of a great many of the lapsed, "knew what a religion ought to look like. It retained the title of ownership after it had left the building" (264).

For Erdozain it is simply not the case that science, whether in Darwinian or cosmological form, was or is the cause of unbelief—although it quickly became atheism's principal symbol and weapon. Notably in the case of the notorious Scopes Trial of 1925, where the point at issue was the propagation of Darwinian principles in schools, the instigator of the protest against a ban on teaching evolution was radicalized when he attended the funeral of a six-year-old son of one of his staff and heard the preacher informing the child's mother that her son was undoubtedly in the flames of hell. Such moments echo the experience of the Welsh millworker cited above.

Moreover an analysis of 150 Victorian freethinkers found that ideas relating to geology or evolution were influential in only three cases. In the words of historian Edward Royle, "Just as Christian belief can be, and often is, founded on an emotional response in a given situation, to be confirmed later by intellectually satisfying 'evidences,' so infidelity seems to have frequently been inspired by disgust with the Church and moral revulsion against Christian doctrines, and then sustained by a growing intellectual conviction of the rightness of such a rejection" (194). Eminent Victorian Benjamin Jowett indicted the false orthodoxy that represented God as "angry with us for what we never did; ready to inflict a disproportionate punishment on us for what we are; satisfied by the sufferings of his son in our stead. The imperfection of human law is transferred to the Divine" (209). George Eliot polished her character Bulstrode in *Middlemarch* to illustrate every worst characteristic of the self-justifying, egoistic, yet piously sincere tyrant that she perceived meticulous Christianity had created.

Erdozain's account models the kind of sustained attention that being with the lapsed requires—in short, an assumption that the reasons for keeping one's distance are genuine, often carefully pondered, likely to be about principled misgivings about the church's ability or willingness to uphold its own moral standards, sometimes troubled by fundamental features of those very standards themselves, and too-frequently triggered by a significant form of rejection or egregious case of censorious exclusion. The lapsed may be epitomized by Ivan Karamazov. In *The Brothers Karamazov* Ivan explains to his brother Aloysha that it's not that he doesn't believe there is a God—it's that he cannot respect a God who allows the suffering of innocent children.

What do I care if the tormentors are in hell, what hell can set right here, if these ones have already been tormented?

... And if the suffering of children goes to make up the sum of suffering needed to buy truth, then I assert beforehand that the whole of truth is not worth such a price.... I don't want harmony, for love of mankind I don't want it. I want to remain with unrequited suffering. I'd rather remain with my unrequited suffering and my unquenched indignation, *even if I am wrong*.... It's not that I don't accept God, Aloysha, I just most respectfully return him the ticket.[3]

Being with the lapsed means having the historical awareness, the humility and the generosity of heart to assume, as a starting point for conversation, that the party in the wrong is likely to be the flock rather than the lost sheep. It's to break through the complacency that assumes the church's abiding benevolence, and to jettison the culture that assures itself of (as Feuerbach pointed out) churchgoers' guaranteed superiority. It's to recognize that the "lapse" is more than likely to have been largely on the church's side. And that the balance of integrity may well be with the lost sheep.

I went to high school in Bristol, on the west coast of England. We all knew Bristol was a beautiful city. But we never seriously asked ourselves what made it beautiful. We all knew Bristol was, comparatively, a wealthy city. But we never seriously pondered what made it wealthy. We all knew Bristol was, in the eighteenth century, the second city in the country, and a magnificent port. But we never enquired what made it so important and prominent. And here's the answer. Between 1730 and 1745, Bristol was the leading slave port in the world. In the course of the eighteenth century around 500,000 slaves provided the profitable goods in the triangular trade between Bristol, West Africa, and the West Indies.

3. Fyodor Dostoyevsky, *The Brothers Karamazov*, trans. Richard Pevear and Larissa Volokonsky (San Francisco: North Point, 1990), 245.

My high school was populated by the children of the wealthy merchants of Bristol. Those merchants made their wealth on the back of slaves crammed into the cargo-holds of transatlantic ships. We were the successors of those merchants. We would never be slaves. We liked to sing the dated and chauvinistic song "Rule, Britannia! Britannia, rule the waves! Britons never, never, never shall be slaves." How ironic that bombastic claim sounds when put in such a context.

One could say, "But this was the society of its day, and not the church." But I went from that high school to study history at university. There I read about Henry Philpotts, who was Bishop of Exeter from 1830–1869. He was not universally popular. Owen Chadwick describes him as "a genuinely religious man with his religion concealed behind porcupine quills," and Sydney Smith lamented, "I must believe in the Apostolic Succession, there being no other way of accounting for the descent of the Bishop of Exeter from Judas Iscariot."[4] He was so fierce in his views on baptismal regeneration that when he refused to institute a clergyman who disagreed with him, he threatened to excommunicate the Archbishop of Canterbury and anyone who supported his disputatious opponent. What I never discovered in my studies, but have more recently learned, is that this giant of the Victorian church, together with three business associates, invested in slave plantations in Jamaica, and when slavery was abolished in the British Empire in 1833 they were paid compensation for the loss of no fewer than 665 slaves.

It is the plethora of such truths about the church's history, and a preponderance of galling stories about its present, that leads Andrew Shanks to believe the church is called to-

---

4. Owen Chadwick, *The Victorian Church*, Part One (London: SCM, 1997), 217; R. S. Lambert, *The Cobbett of the West* (London: Nicholson & Watson Limited, 1939), 39.

day to adjust its sense of its identity and mission and to seek to become a pioneeringly honest ex-oppressor community.[5] The lapsed include those who may perhaps have slunk away in shame or whose life changed course because they, like the character Prendergast in Evelyn Waugh's novel *Decline and Fall*, had doubts for no apparent reason.[6] But if the church is looking to rediscover its mission it can do so by assuming the lapsed, more often than not, have seen something the flock urgently need to see. Thus by being with the lapsed it can learn to become more aware of its shortcomings, more realistic about its true nature, and more resolved to become such a pioneeringly honest ex-oppressor community.

Lest attention yield no more than gloomy self-excoriation, **mystery, delight,** and **enjoyment** offer a response rooted in the words of Peter (quoting Ps. 118), "the stone that was rejected by you, the builders; it has become the cornerstone" (Acts 4:11). Mystery and delight chart a journey from repentance to renewal, which goes as follows.

Many people have, in their early life, stood in the playground at elementary school while two captains picked sides for a competitive team game. There's a fight over who will be captains and then there are celebrations and disappointments as good players are separated into teams. Then, invariably, comes the moment, as the better players become impatient to start, while the stragglers are still waiting to be picked, when one of the captains says the words, "I'll have her, and (with a dismissive sweep of the hand), you can have the rest." The "rest" are those whose talents are to be regarded as negligible, such that no one much cares whose side they're on. Such a dismissive sweep of the hand can be the defining

5. Andrew Shanks, "Honesty," in *Praying for England: Priestly Presence in Contemporary Culture*, ed. Samuel Wells and Sarah Coakley (London and New York: Continuum, 2008), 125–45.

6. Evelyn Waugh, *Decline and Fall* (London: Penguin, 1928).

point of a person's life. It marks a person as the stone that the builders rejected. Either you fight the rejection and risk being seen as a person who just doesn't get it, or you accept the rejection and assume the identity of someone whom the world would be better off without.

One pastor worked in a community for several years where one of the leaders once said, "You know, we're a bunch of misfits who somehow fit together." What the leader was recognizing was that, rather than rebelling against feelings of rejection, the community had found if it worked constructively with those feelings it could become something rather beautiful. People in the wider conversation began to use the word "inclusion" but that community didn't believe inclusion was really the right word. It mistrusted the word "inclusion" because it seemed to suggest there were a bunch of people in the center whose lives were normal and sorted and privileged, and that those people should jolly well open the doors and welcome people in and be a bit more thoughtful and kind and generous. The community regarded this as a patronizing and paternalistic model. When the community leader said, "We're a bunch of misfits who somehow fit together," he wasn't regarding himself as normal and secure and somehow above it all: he was well aware he was one of the misfits too. He was reframing the whole idea that there was a center and a periphery, where the center gave kindly hospitality to the periphery—because he perceived the cost of that idea was that the periphery feels humiliated and the center feels smug.

Mystery, delight, and enjoyment name the discovery that, if you're looking for a cornerstone, the best place to look is among the stones that the builders have rejected. One congregation held a number of events around dementia and faith. At one such evening what electrified the room was when a person with dementia and a person caring for a loved one with dementia each spoke with wisdom, courage, and truth. Those with dementia are among the stones most rejected, but that night it was brilliantly obvious that the Holy Spirit was speaking through them. One disability event began with a person with autism describing in unforgettable detail what it would have felt like for a person like him to be present in the crowd at the first Palm Sunday, and how the sensory overload would have overwhelmed him. No one listening could ever see all the hosannas and palm branches in such an innocent way again. The same congregation also hosted an event for single people in which participants explored the advantages and disappointments, sadness and opportunity of being voluntarily or involuntarily single. Again it was a discovery of solidarity, wisdom, and hope. On another occasion there was an event for those fleeing oppressive societies on account of their sexual identity. These were stones the builders had rejected if one ever saw them: but coming together in the company of others who'd been rejected in different ways, they could find inspiration and purpose beyond fear and escape. In each case these rejected stones could easily be—and in many cases, at earlier times in their lives, had been—the lapsed; but, vitally, people had been with them, attended to them, seen them as mysteries not problems, and enjoyed them: and so they became the cornerstone.

The crucial step in being with the lapsed is, personally—or, better, collectively—to make the journey to realizing that the Bible was written by people who discovered that they were the stone the builders rejected—and thus to understand what it feels like to be rejected. Israel was in Babylon, in exile, captured and deported by the Chaldeans, dragged a thousand miles due east. It was angry, guilty, depressed, despairing, doubtful, paralyzed, powerless. And what Israel did was to piece together the half-remembered stories of its people from a thousand years before, stories of slavery, escape, and freedom. Most crucial of all were the stories at the heart of the narrative, stories of the time in the wilderness when slavery was a memory but true freedom was still out of reach. These stories were crucial because that was how Israel was feeling in a new wilderness called Babylon, in a desolate season called exile. They were discovering what it means to feel you're the stone the builders rejected. The exiles in Babylon wrote down their people's wilderness history because it had important lessons for their own present and future. And what they came to realize was that they were closer to God in exile than they'd ever been in the promised land. That's the discovery on which the whole Bible rests.

Congregations often think they need to be full of big and strong and powerful people. But Jesus was the stone the builders rejected; and in his ministry he surrounded himself with stones that the builders had rejected. Jesus didn't found the church on the so-called center—the sorted, the normal, the benevolent and condescending. Jesus assumed the church would always need the work of the Holy Spirit—the work of miracle, of subversion, of turning the world upside-down. Nothing has changed—except for a lot of the intervening years the church has forgotten who Jesus was and whose company he kept. It is not that the church is the good shepherd and the lapsed are the lost sheep; it is more that the stone that the builders rejected is Jesus—and the stones the church has rejected may turn out to be Jesus too.

Thus mystery, delight, and enjoyment don't simply offer a bland and affirming insight that a lot of people who've been overlooked in life turn out to have some important things to contribute. That's true, but what Peter sees in Acts chapter 4 is rather more radical than that. The stone that the builders rejected didn't find a place in the wall somewhere by being thoughtfully included like a last-minute addition to a family photo. The rejected stone became the *cornerstone*, the keystone—the stone that held up all the others, the crucial link, the vital connection. That's what being with the lapsed is all about—not condescendingly making welcome alienated strangers, but seeking out the lapsed and rejected precisely because they are the energy and the life-force that will transform the whole community. Every pastor, every missionary, every evangelist, and every disciple should have these words over their desk, over their windscreen, on their screensaver, in the photo section of their wallet, wherever they see it all the time—"the stone the builders rejected has become the cornerstone." Put another way, "If you're looking for where the future church is coming from, look at what the church and society has so blithely rejected." Being with the lapsed is about constantly recognizing the sin of how much we have rejected, and celebrating the grace that God gives us back what we once rejected in order for it to become the cornerstone of our lives. That's what incarnational mission means.

On the night before he died Peter rejected Jesus. He denied him three times. Jesus was the stone Peter rejected. But Peter became the stone, the rock on which the church was founded, and Jesus, the rejected one, became the keystone. This is the central mystery. Jesus is the stone that the builders rejected. And Peter was one of those builders. But Jesus renamed Peter the stone, and in so doing made him the cornerstone: this is delight. The church is founded on and comprised of stones that the builders rejected. Being with the lapsed means learning to see Jesus in the face of the ones we have rejected; and letting the Jesus we discover in them become our cornerstone. This is enjoyment.

To enjoy the lapsed is not to calculate the usefulness they can be to oneself but to rejoice in the wonder of what they are in themselves. To delight in the lapsed is not to lament for (or criticize) what they have not been but to anticipate and relish what they can be.

Here, as often, the distinction between **participation** and **partnership** is helpful. Partnership says, "These are the specific ways in which your absence diminishes our community; these are the precise skills you would (and used to) bring, the interests you would foster, the concerns you would encourage, the questions you would ask, the energy you would add, the love you would share, the song you would sing, the challenges you would raise, the insights you would offer. Meanwhile, may we tell you, with all due humility, about some things we wonder whether you currently have in the way you would be exposed to and would experience and enjoy with us." (If this second list is succinct then the community may already have learned its lesson.) Most people like to be needed, provided that neediness and its demands don't become disproportionate, disrespectful, or demeaning; it's important for a community to be one of interdependence where everyone both meets need and is able to articulate weakness. People can leave communities out of self-preservation when the needs are too great, or out of hurt when their contribution is overlooked or taken for granted. The conversation with the lapsed about partnership, particularly if that conversation takes place with a congregation leader, may simply involve the words, "I recognize now that we didn't pay attention to you—we didn't see you or didn't delight in you or enjoy you; but we see you now and we realize what you could bring to our community." In such a way partnership names a further aspect in which being with the lapsed advances the renewal of the community.

But participation says something apparently more direct and unsophisticated: "We miss you. Life is about with—and without you, there hasn't been any with this last season. We really could use the things you'd bring, and we really do think you'd be enriched by being part of our community again—but those aren't the deepest reasons we've come searching for you. The real reason is that you're unique. God made you this way because God wanted one like you, and we see that uniqueness too. And we don't feel we're who we're called to be unless you're with us—in fact we don't feel we can fully be with each other and with God unless you're a part of that with. And we realize that you rejoining us may require some genuine learning and real change on our part; perhaps some repentance and reparation too."

Thus does awareness of the absence of one member of the body presage the renewal in mission and ministry of the whole church. Such is the gift of the lapsed.

CHAPTER 2

Being with Seekers

If being with the lapsed is a humble exercise in attention and partnership, inspired by glory, then being with seekers is a practice of delight and participation, inspired by enjoyment. Being with the lapsed can be a sobering realization of how much the church has let people down and fallen short of what God calls it to be. Being with seekers is more often a refreshing reminder of the wonder of God, an iridescence that's more than capable of shining through the shortcomings of the church. The lapsed are those who once looked to the church and its representatives to mediate their relationship with God and now no longer do—either because they no longer believe there's a God to be mediated or because they no longer trust the church's power or moral claim to do so. Seekers are those who have not (or have not for a long time) looked to the church to mediate their relationship with God but are beginning to do so—either because they are drawn to the church and are open to the glory to which the church professes to point, or because they are drawn to God and are looking for a tradition and a community through which that calling can find companions and direction. In passing it's worth noting that some people might be described as either lapsed or seekers; people who have had significant exposure to church life as children but have not come as young adults to make it their own might be one example.

The question of **presence** is a subtle one because "seeker" is a designation one may give to people, but few would use it to describe themselves. If most seekers came looking for disciples to draw them into faith, being with seekers would best be described as ministry rather than mission. But most do not—or, if they do, don't acknowledge, least of all to themselves, that that's what they're doing. Which makes presence all the more significant. Some who see their ministry as primarily to seekers speak of "loitering with intent" when referring to the incarnational commitment to linger around the coffee machine, make conversation on the bus, or talk to the other parents watching the children's ball game. The intent is not so much to force convictions on an unwary conversation partner as to be constantly open to any topic of discussion yielding an area of tenderness, wondering, inquiry, or appetite for faith that may trigger a dialogue of real significance. It goes without saying that seekers are more likely to trust the counsel of those they already know rather than a stranger; but few people change their heart and mind based on one conversation or relationship alone. It's not so much about one person having one interchange that alters everything: it's much more about a series of experiences and conversations that together draw a person from a general sense of seeking to a more focused desire to find—or be found. Thus does presence turn into **partnership**.

One pastor never really understood colleagues who would begin the worship service with announcements. She felt it jarred liturgically to start by referring to things that were due to happen at another time and often another place. It seemed a strange form of hospitality to get bogged down in the housekeeping arrangements before offering what the newcomers thought they'd come for. And, in practical terms, the earnest injunctions to join in with things would invariably be issued when a third of the congregation were yet to arrive.

So she preferred to make the announcements part of the way the service would end—a bit like the advertisements that come between the climax of the sit-com and the final scene. She noted the unswerving law of church that, while people don't much listen to announcements, they do reserve the right to take profound offense at them. She was aware of pastors who pore over every semicolon of a sermon text—but assume that, when it comes to the announcements, they can just "wing it." Which is how, with clumsy attempts at humor, dismissive remarks about the youth program, or forgetting to thank the flower arrangers, pastors frequently end up revealing rather more than they intended to. And often take much too long in doing so.

One Sunday, having highlighted the worthy lecture and issued the weary call for volunteers, that same pastor said, "You know, I should probably say this every Sunday, but if you've come this morning feeling brokenhearted or ever-so-anxious about something, don't leave without talking to one of the pastors about it. You know that's why we have coffee hour—to get to know each other well enough that, when it all falls apart, we can share what we're going through. And don't start by saying 'I know you're terribly busy.' Because talking to you is what we're here for."

So she had no one to blame but herself when the first person out the door skipped the "Lovely service" pleasantries and just came straight out with it. "I get the God part," he said; "I just can't connect with the Jesus part." That was it. No worries about a husband showing early signs of dementia, no agony over a brother's divorce, no torment over a whistleblowing scenario at work. Someone was saying that the biggest issue in their life—something they were desperate to talk to someone about, even a pastor (they were that desperate)—was actually about God. So the pastor said the first thing that came into her head. "I think Jesus is God saying, 'I'm not far away and long ago and theoretical: I'm here and now and in your face.' Do you want a God who's a nice idea, or a God who's about everything now and forever?" The man in the greeting line said, "The everything God." The pastor said, "Then I think you do get the Jesus part." And then the man left. The pastor wondered if she would ever know if the man wanted an answer or would have preferred a listening ear.

A couple of people further down the line looked at the pastor meaningfully, as if they were trying maybe to ask, or perhaps to tell, but couldn't find courage or words. No one said much, until it came to the last person out the door. He'd clearly made sure he was the last person. He said (remarkable as this may seem, it's a true story), "I get the Jesus part. I just can't get the God part." The pastor was even more dumbfounded than the first time. To meet one person in the heartsearchings of faith might be a wonder; but to get two made her think perhaps they'd had a bet and were pulling her leg. But this second man was perfectly genuine. And this wasn't a passing exchange at the door; this one had hung back for a real sit-down conversation. Which ensued.

The pastor started thinking, "Is this the same conversation as earlier—or is it the opposite?" It was hard to tell. Slightly regretting her knee-jerk response a few moments earlier, this time she just listened. What emerged fairly quickly was a tale of touching humility from a person whose early formation had been narrow and dogmatic and who was quick to write off his experience as inadequate and his faith as insufficient. In the end the pastor said this: "At the beginning you said you didn't get God. You got Jesus, the sacrificial love, the open-hearted inclusion, the never letting us go; but you didn't get God.

"But you've told me a story of memory, and gratitude, and awe, and hope. Honestly, if you had to describe Christianity in four words, you could do a lot worse than 'memory,' 'gratitude,' 'awe,' and 'hope.' I think the only place I'd gently challenge you is to wonder why we don't see you here more often: because those are hard words to live on your own. If you were part of a community that shares the struggle with these words, you'd make the rather rueful discovery that most churchgoers aren't as far along on the life of memory, gratitude, awe, and hope as you are.

"And by the way, that God you mentioned earlier, the one you didn't get—the one you said was somewhere beyond sacrificial love, open-hearted inclusion, and never letting us go. I don't get that God either. I think if you get Jesus, you get pretty much all the God there is."

Then they sat in silence together the way you only do with someone you're really close to. What her companion was thinking, the pastor realized she might never know. What she was thinking was, "If only we dared ask what was in the hearts of those who walk in the doors of the church. If only we dared hope that faith really was the most important thing in people's lives. Those two people who risked saying what they really thought have just taught me what it means to be a pastor."

This is a story of partnerships because without the pastor's words during the announcements these two seekers might not have articulated how close they were to faith; but it was for the seekers, not the pastor, to make the rest of the journey. It was something that couldn't be done for them; they had to do it for themselves. There was wisdom and experience the pastor could bring from other times and other places, from an understanding of years spent as a steward of the mysteries of God; but the real work remained to be done by the seekers themselves, and the conversations, one brief, one longer, were largely about teasing out what that work was and whether they were respectively interested in doing it.

Being with seekers can be a genuine **delight** only if both parties recognize and relish the fact that they are entering unknown territory. It's not that Christianity is a given body of doctrine and practice to which seekers get gradually closer and closer before adopting wholesale. It's that faith is a relationship with God and with the church and that a new set of eyes, and a new heart and soul, bring fresh perspective, alternative insight, and new energy to that relationship. The church grows by conversion—not just numerically, but spiritually, intellectually, and experientially.

Seekers are those who "get the Jesus bit, but don't get the God bit," or "get the God bit, but don't get the Jesus bit," or "get the church bit, but don't get the God bit," or "get the God bit, but don't get the church bit." Some people have a benign sense of providence, a deep respect for creation, but don't associate those sentiments with a personal God or a committed community. Others have a profound thirst for and/ or experience of intimate relationship, but they don't connect that with a cosmic reality or a lived fellowship. Others again have a healthy sense of the value and virtues of regular communal support and sharing, but they don't instinctively connect that with a God who made the heavens or who longs to be with them in Christ. Such people need faith, formation, church—but they also need each other: for not only may they quickly discover how complementary their dispositions are, but if they stay around a congregation for any length of time they'll also find that it's made up of the same diversity of starting points.

Delight means both rejoicing in the gift of this new person—their questions, their story, their experience, their innocence—and at the same time celebrating anew the faith they are encountering—its surprises, its eccentricities, its absurdities, its grace, its truth. Evangelism seldom involves a fusillade of persuasive arguments or a prepared package of attractive promises. It is largely about trusting the Holy Spirit, delighting in the seeker, and creating an environment where the Holy Spirit can best work. If you delight in someone, you want to know more about them; you want to know what they're good at, what they're passionate about, what they do for fun, what they think is worth doing for its own sake. And then you want to know what really matters to them, and what the story of that concern is, and where the tender areas are, and how they have encountered and addressed adversity in their life. But you also want them to meet your friends, to introduce you to what excites them, to respect and explore what means most to you. If your faith is genuine, such exchanges will expose it to the light, and it will communicate itself. Of course there is information—about the Bible, doctrine, ethics, worship, discipleship, the planned giving scheme—but invariably it's not this framework of faith and practice that turns a seeker into a disciple: it's relationship—the relationship with someone who takes delight in them, and the window that relationship opens on the God who takes delight in them.

Delight becomes **participation** at precisely the moment the seeker realizes this isn't an instrumental relationship— that they're not a head to be counted, a trophy to be held aloft, a conquest to be boasted of. There is joy in heaven. Becoming known by the children of earth is God's greatest delight. For a host of reasons there's likely to be suspicion to break down. Many people have never known a non-instrumental relationship, except perhaps within the family; very often not even there. One pastor went to see the mother of a fourteen-year-old boy who had recently spent a good deal of time amid the church community. The mother was skeptical: "I told him,

'They just want your money.'" The pastor responded, "One day we will want his money—if and when he has any. But we'll never be more eager to receive his money than he is to give it. And when that moment comes, he won't be giving it away, he'll be returning it to the one he believes it truly belongs to, because he trusts that God knows better what's good for him than he does himself." The mother wasn't persuaded. The point was her son was set on joining a community of faith, but in doing so it would remain, from her point of view, "them"; for him, it would be "us" because his voice would count, his views would matter, and he would have a say in how that money was spent. The area of tension wouldn't be that "they" wanted his money (all parties knew that he, and she, had little or no money)—it would be that this new "us" would challenge, rival, and transform the "us" that his mother had previously assumed was hers alone.

For that is the heart of participation with seekers. If this Christian thing is more than a curiosity, if it's deeper than a pastime and beyond an intuition, if it really does demand your soul, your life, your all, then there will be no relationship it doesn't affect, no habit or duty it doesn't modify, no convention or tradition it doesn't transform. Conversion is a transvaluation of all values. It's not possible, necessary, or helpful to deny, devalue, or dissemble about that: what's needed is companionship—a sense that others appreciate, understand, and have patience with how challenging it can be to take an audit of all aspects of life in the light of the gospel. Again, this should be a point of renewal for the companion of the seeker; for such an audit behooves any Christian at any stage in life. Being with a seeker means accompanying them as they take stock of what it means to become a disciple ("Or what king, going out to wage war against another king, will not sit down first and consider whether he is able with ten thousand to oppose the one who comes against him with twenty thousand?," Luke 14:31) and remembering that it takes just as much care and commitment to remain a disciple as to become one ("No one who puts a hand to the plow and looks back is fit," Luke 9:62).

Part of what participation affirms is that this is not something that anyone can do on the seeker's behalf. Likewise it's not something that can be rushed. As ever, participation requires a good deal of patience. This is the territory of **attention**. Everyone's journey to faith is different, everyone's obstacles and fears and unfinished business are different. Why does the question of God and suffering become a sticking point? Probably not as an intellectual question—more likely because a close relative went through hell and it would seem to be betraying that relative to become a disciple without pausing to address the suffering question in detail. Why is the issue of other faiths so pressing? Again, probably not as a general query about the existence of people of integrity who believe so differently, but more likely because a much-cared-for friend or family member is an adherent of another faith and what they will make of this new development remains unknown. Being with the seeker is about taking time to understand the complexity of what conversion means and acknowledging its cost as well as its promise.

One pastor was a little bewildered by a woman on the edge of faith who appeared at his church around once a year. Once they'd had lunch at a prestigious restaurant in the town, and the pastor had learned that there'd been one marriage, productive of many offspring but nonetheless short-lived; and there was a view of church that seemed full of fear and anxious of shame. Some years later they found themselves at a grand lunch a second time—she, still gazing mistrustfully at the pastor, as if imagining he might up and leave at any moment; the pastor, wondering how he'd got himself tangled in a ball of wool, not knowing what this was really all about.

The conversation sallied around assorted issues of the day. Then suddenly, without any warning, she announced she had a question to ask—the kind of question that's introduced with a silence that has the same effect as a drum-roll. "Do you believe the Archbishop of Canterbury was correct when, in 1954, he told Princess Margaret that she should not marry Group Captain Peter Townsend?"

That was the question; the one on which everything, it seemed, was to rest. A question about an event more than a half-century earlier; an event that involved the Queen's sister, who had a celebrated love affair with a senior servant of the royal household, but, since her lover was divorced, came to the conclusion (with more than a little help from her sister and the political and ecclesiastical heavyweights of the era) that she would not accept his proposal of marriage. This was the question it had taken several years of acquaintance for this seeker to articulate; the question, it seemed, that her lugubrious social dance, her Esther-like extension of one banquet invitation to another, had been all a maneuver to elicit. The pastor was at a loss. He started to piece together clues, like Hercule Poirot amassing circumstantial evidence: she was very nervous about asking me; she seemed to identify with the Princess's notorious unhappiness in love; while long, long ago, the Princess's story must have been fresh in the mind when her own marriage was breaking down.

The pastor was beginning to make some progress when— her attention on his response unwavering, her breathless waiting for his answer urgent—she stepped in with the crucial clarifying detail. "After my marriage failed," she said, "my husband asked me for a divorce. I think he'd met someone else. But I was brought up to believe that marriage was indissoluble. So, even though there wasn't any prospect of a reconciliation, I said no. And he took his own life." The pastor's stomach lurched. He nodded to indicate, silently, "It's ok. I can do the rest." He left a considerable pause to register that he appreciated the enormity of what she was saying.

He had to say it out loud. There was nowhere to hide. "Does it feel like you've based your whole life, your whole understanding of God, and your whole family's unhappiness, on a mistake?" The seeker held the pastor's gaze. "Yes," she replied.

The pastor saw, with unprecedented clarity, all the honest, genuine, and earnest ways the church seeks to lead people in the paths of righteousness, and how absurd, how damaging, and how tragic some of those paths seem a generation or two later. This woman looked at the pastor with all the fear, all the pain, and all the trust the church has instilled in people all these centuries. Who had been wrong? The clergy of Princess Margaret's day for upholding what church and society both took for granted was good and right and true? This woman for living a life of obedience when the evidence of the eyes and her heart told her otherwise? Or the pastor's generation for jettisoning the strictures of those that had gone before and having such confidence in the justice and humanity of its own perceptions?

There's not much to say when you sit at lunch and your companion is coming to the realization that the last fifty years of her life have been based on a mistake. The pastor scratched around for what to utter next. But words were not required. The seeker wasn't angry. She almost looked relieved. The pastor hadn't answered her question. She'd answered it herself. Maybe that was the mistake the archbishop made in 1954. He'd assumed ministry was about providing answers, guidance, direction. All the pastor had done over lunch was not to leave the table till his companion had found the courage to face the truth. That's what being with is. For this seeker, until the central stumbling block was addressed, nothing in life could change. But once it had, everything was possible. Such are the opportunities opened up by being with and paying close attention.

It's a short step from here to **mystery**. There are plenty of examples in the Gospels and Acts of those who are intrigued by Jesus—some of whom want things entirely on their terms, like Nicodemus, Herod Antipas, or Pilate, others of whom want to come close but waver on the brink, like Simon the Pharisee or the rich young man, others of whom again relish delight and participation and respond enthusiastically, like Zacchaeus or the Ethiopian eunuch, or respond to actions that speak louder than words, like the centurion who pleads for his servant or the centurion at the cross. Mystery lies in what draws one person to Christ and another away. For example, the account of the two thieves at the cross portrays one whose suffering and shame brought him to seek mercy and reconciliation, another for whom punishment and agony evoked bitterness and anger. Of the seven healed lepers, one, a Samaritan, returned and gave thanks; the others were never seen again. Joseph of Arimathea, at huge cost to himself, provided spices and a fresh tomb; whereas others of the Sanhedrin, it seems, saw Jesus solely as a threat and a danger. What draws people to Christ is the mystery of grace; but the mystery of sin, of ignorance or perversity, is a greater mystery, not in scale but in irrationality, not in depth but in purposelessness.

Alongside the mystery of how some are drawn while others refrain, is the mystery of coming to faith itself. What Paul calls "new creation" and elsewhere the discovery that "it is not I who live but Christ who lives in me" is scarcely the work of the seeker at all, but the definitive place where one steps aside—even in regard to one's own identity and destiny—and the Holy Spirit does the rest. Chains fall off, hearts become free, resurrection happens, response is triggered, following ensues. This is by no means always or usually sudden, or even all at the same time; but being with the seeker means anticipating—yet still being surprised and delighted by—the wondrous things God can do in the life of a person who ceases to oppose them. And this is **glory**—not the triumph a salesperson gets when a customer decides to buy a car, nor the thrill a suitor feels when an alluring companion accepts an invitation on a date, but an epiphany of Easter morning—a step from death to life, from despair to hope, more like the birth of a baby: a new beginning of limitless possibility.

Together, delight and participation should model a true sense of **enjoyment**. For the journey from seeker to disciple is itself a transformation from one who uses God and the church to one who enjoys them. The seeker uses God and the church in the sense that they remain options among an array of possible directions; they may be agreeable, appealing, or congenial in some conditions, circumstances, or moods, but they have no overarching authority that makes them compelling in all events. There remains an opt-out clause, a release button should church prove too cloying, controlling, or uncouth, or should God prove too demanding, confusing, or distant. To the extent that God and church remain one choice among alternatives, they are being used rather than enjoyed. But at the point the seeker becomes a disciple, God and church cease to be provisional: they become the reality around which other (previously given) elements become contingent.

In similar fashion the experience of becoming a disciple should be of entering, perhaps for the first time, a culture in which one is enjoyed rather than used. It may be that in the rest of life—in all other relationships both today and historically—the seeker realizes that they have been used; they've been a means to an end, valued for what ancillary blessing they could bring or lever, regarded for what advantage or skill they could offer or implement—but never cherished in themselves. A church community, if it's being what it should be, straightforwardly enjoys the new disciple for what they alone are and the gift they uniquely constitute. As with participation, enjoyment requires patience. Some people remain seekers for most of their lives: the step into discipleship never comes for them, or comes after a long period of uncertainty and many misgivings. Enjoyment means cherishing such a person just as much as one would cherish a new disciple. They are no less valued for the fact that they can't find the words, the feelings, the conviction—after all, faith is a gift, not an achievement, and it's absurd to think less of someone if they've not been given that gift. Which means, finally, that being with seekers is an occasion for gratitude—for the gift that they are, and for the gift of faith, which, when and if it comes, is a pearl beyond price.

CHAPTER 3

Being with Those of No Professed Faith

This, the central of the first five chapters, is the hardest to categorize. Mission means being with all those who have taken the freedom of God's patience not yet to believe. Some did believe, and no longer do—they are the lapsed. Some would like to believe, but have not yet found a way in—they are the seekers. Some have faith convictions, but shaped around another story and another community, perhaps similar, maybe very different—they are those of other faiths. Some are defined perhaps overmuch by what they don't believe, and see Christianity in particular, or religion in general, as the source of the world's problems, seeking to extirpate it by argument or more active means. They are the hostile. But what of the others? They are, in some cultures, the majority. They are those whose lives are not characterized by religious observance, who do not locate themselves in a narrative that Christians would recognize as similar or parallel to their own. They don't have a collective identity, or common characteristics. Christians only know them by what they are not—they are those of no professed faith. It's not that they are believing without belonging—subscribing to some parts of a Trinitarian perspective in spirituality, doctrine, and ethics: that would make them either lapsed or seekers. It's not that they actively or more passively disagree with Christianity, believing it should be resisted, its rivals given more public credibility, or its real or apparent social privilege dismantled: that would make them hostile. It's that in a world where people, on the whole, live and let live, Christianity has no significant part in their life, for good or ill.

Being with those of no professed faith begins with the **mystery** that is the sheer incongruity and incomprehensibility of unbelief. George Hunsinger describes carefully the contrast between Karl Barth, who thought of the real and the unreal, and Reinhold Niebuhr, who contrasted the real with the ideal. For Niebuhr, love was unattainable, but the very fact of its unattainability ensured that thinkers recalled the sinfulness and fallibility of achievements and institutions. Thus Niebuhr described love as an "impossible possibility." Sin was real: love was ideal. For Barth, God was the definition of what could be called real—and anything that stood against the reality of God was unreal. Thus for Barth, the "impossible possibility" was not love, but sin. "Sin's origin was inexplicable, its status was deeply conflicted, and its destiny was to vanish." Only paradoxical language could describe what was indeed genuinely there and must unavoidably be taken into account, but was, in essence, absurd—being "an impossible possibility and an unreal reality."[1] Being of no professed faith is, for Christians, such an inexplicable reality, such an unfathomable but nonetheless undeniable state of existence: a mystery.

Given that what is being offered is grace—limitless love, unbounded forgiveness, eternal companionship, utter

---

1. George Hunsinger, *How to Read Karl Barth: The Shape of His Theology* (New York: Oxford University Press, 1991), 38–39.

fulfillment, thorough vindication in the face of injustice, unconstrained redemption of all that has been lost to time, ignorance, folly, or misadventure, true reconciliation with all from whom one has been estranged—who could possibly say no? There's a story, popular in Ireland, of the man who is visited by a fairy godmother and granted three wishes. He didn't have to think long about the first wish. "I'd like a glass of Guinness that refills as soon as I drink it," he said. Sure enough, his wish was granted. After he'd enjoyed a couple of drinks and found the glass kept replenishing, the fairy godmother said to him, "Don't forget you've got two more wishes." The man looked at the constantly refilling glass and said, "I'll have two more of those please." When you have truly found what makes your heart sing, there's no need to search or speculate about much else.

When Jesus says, "I am the bread of life. Whoever comes to me will never be hungry, and whoever believes in me will never be thirsty," how could anyone walk away? This is the good news. Jesus breaks bread, and there is more than enough for everybody. Then Jesus lays down his life, and himself becomes the living bread, broken for the life of the world. Yet even Jesus's death is not wasted, and his resurrection offers us the promise that we shall eat this bread with him forever. It seems from John 6 that there are two reasons people walk away. One is that Jesus is too ordinary. The universe is massive and staggeringly complex. Sometimes it does seem curious to say it all comes down to this solitary historical figure two thousand years ago. The second reason is the opposite: he's too far-fetched. He's too demanding—too extraordinary. Everything's relative—no promises last forever, no truth claims go much beyond rhetoric and some kind of bid for power, no one gets to have a monopoly on what's important. Peter doesn't deny these two false avenues: he simply says, "Lord, to whom can we go? You have the words of eternal life." When you've seen what we've seen, discovered what we've discovered, shared what we've shared, tasted what we've tasted—nothing compares to you. Anything else is absurd.

Thus the simplicity and stubbornness of the conviction that the Jesus who said "I am the bread of life" is the life of the world, that whoever comes to him will never be hungry and whoever believes in him will never be thirsty, even if they couldn't care less at the moment. One pastor served a demanding charge in a region where faith, if it existed, seldom translated into churchgoing. There were Sunday mornings when he would arrive at 9:30 a.m. for the 11:00 a.m. service, set out the chairs and everything else, and wait. And sometimes at 10:55 a.m. he would still be the only one there, longing for someone to come and share the bread of life. He would wonder what he was doing, holding out for Jesus when no one seemed to want him. And the words of Peter were the words that kept him going: "Lord, to whom can we go? You have the words of eternal life."

At such moments that pastor was inspired by identifying with what it means for God to be bewildered by unbelief—so deftly expressed by the poet Richard Crashaw:

I am all-fair, yet no one loveth me:
Noble, yet no one would my servant be:
Rich, yet no suppliant at my gate appears:
Almighty, yet before me no one fears:
Eternal, I by very few am sought:
Wise am I, yet my counsel goes for nought:
I am the way, yet by me walks scarce one:
The truth, why am I not relied upon?
The life, yet seldom one my help requires:
The true light, yet to see me none desires:
And I am merciful, yet none is known

To place his confidence in me alone.
Man, if thou perish, 'tis that thou dost choose it;
Salvation I have wrought for thee, O use it![2]

For Blaise Pascal, the category of those of no professed faith makes no sense. "There are only two kinds of people one can call reasonable: those who serve God with all their heart because they know Him, and those who seek Him with all their heart because they do not know Him"—or what I am calling disciples and seekers.[3] In Pascal's view, the prospect of one's own impending death governs the rational person's whole perspective about the question of faith.

> We do not require great education of the mind to under-stand that here is no real and lasting satisfaction; that our pleasures are only vanity; that our evils are infinite; and, lastly, that death, which threatens us every moment, must infallibly place us within a few years under the dreadful necessity of being forever either annihilated or unhappy. (#194, p. 47)

Pascal struggles to maintain respect for those who seem im-pervious to the jeopardy in which their eternal well-being lies, and content to go to their deaths ignorant of whether they will spend forever in oblivion or misery. Pascal simply cannot comprehend it:

---

2. Richard Crashaw, "Jesus Christ's Expostulation with an Ungrate-ful World," in *Complete Works of Richard Crashaw c. 1613–1649* (London: Robson and Sons). See https://archive.org/stream/complete02cras/ complete02cras_djvu.txt.

3. Blaise Pascal, *Pascal's Pensées*, with an introduction by T. S. Eliot (New York: Dutton, 1958), #194, p. 49. Hereafter, references are given in parentheses in the text.

Nothing is so important to man as his own state, nothing is
so formidable to him as eternity; and thus it is not natural
that there should be men indifferent to the loss of their
existence, and to the perils of everlasting suffering. They
are quite different with regard to all other things. They are
afraid of mere trifles; they foresee them; they feel them.
And this same man who spends so many days and nights
in rage and despair for the loss of office, or for some imag-
inary insult to his honor, is the very one who knows without anxiety and without emotion that he will lose all by
death. (#194, p. 48)

Even if one had little regard for one's eternal well-being,
Pascal speculates, surely one would have a care for how one
is perceived by others in this life. Pascal takes for granted that
"the only way to succeed in this life is to make ourselves appear honorable, faithful, judicious, and capable of useful service to a friend; because naturally men love only what may
be useful to them" (#194, p. 48). Should one wager that there
is a God, even if one turns out to be wrong, one will nonetheless be "faithful, honest, humble, grateful, generous, a sincere
friend, truthful" (#233, p. 56).

Pascal allows that one may imagine oneself to be the
sole master of one's conduct, and accountable for it only to
oneself; but he can't imagine how such a view, particularly
advanced in a boasting and haughty spirit, would make anyone look to such a person for consolation, advice, or help.
Such things, if sincerely held, are not to be said cheerfully,
but sadly—as the saddest thing in the world. He doesn't deny
the ambiguity of existence: he simply cannot begin to understand how or why a person might feel able to withhold judgment on it—as he puts it, "You must wager. It is not optional.
You are embarked" (#233, p. 55). But ambiguity nonetheless
abides, even after Christ's incarnation.

It was not then right that He should appear in a manner manifestly divine, and completely capable of convincing all men; but it was also not right that He should come in so hidden a manner that He could not be known by those who should sincerely seek Him. He has willed to make Himself quite recognizable by those; and thus, willing to appear openly to those who seek Him with all their heart, and to be hidden from those who flee from Him with all their heart, He so regulates the knowledge of Himself that He has given signs of Himself visible to those who seek Him, and not to those who seek Him not. (#430, p. 91)

Thus in faith there is enough light for those who want to believe and enough shadows to blind those who don't. By saying this, and while seeking to dismantle and discredit what he sees as the complacency of agnosticism, Pascal allows for the possibility of genuine atheism.

In the process he touches on what many today would see as the almost inevitable symptom of agnosticism—idolatry. The issue of idolatry rests on how or whether it's possible not actually to believe in anything. Not so much how it's possible psychologically to sustain life amid so much ambiguity; more a recognition of how much of life depends on trust, habit, and shared understanding, and whether these are not in fact the chief constituents of faith. Do people who claim not to believe in anything truly not rest their existence significantly on trust, habit, and shared understanding—and would a portrayal of faith that did not ground it in such things not render it a caricature? The determination not to believe in anything becomes idolatry when one surveys the substitutes for faith—the things in which people do place their most passionate and sustained trust, habit, and shared understanding—and finds they turn out to be things unworthy of such exaltation, such as their dwelling place, a sports team, or a particular way of making ale. Pascal calls those of no professed faith—what he terms "the doubter who does not seek"—indescribably silly; given that "they judge themselves so little worthy of their own care," he maintains that "they are unworthy of the care of others"; and the believer must therefore "call upon them to have pity on themselves" (#194, pp. 47–49).

It's possible to share in Barth's and Pascal's bewilderment about the mystery of unbelief and not endorse Pascal's rather abrasive view of the agnostic. After all, Pascal perceived that there were three sources of belief—reason, custom, and inspiration—and that only inspiration could produce "a true and saving effect" (#245, p. 59). He was a person of balance: "If we submit everything to reason, our religion will have no mysterious and supernatural element. If we offend the principles of reason, our religion will be absurd and ridiculous" (#273, p. 63). Being with those of no professed faith means acknowledging and not suppressing one's bafflement at the plausibility of unbelief but at the same time attaining a level of humility and grace in the face of it that Pascal seldom articulates.

To say, "For your own sake, I believe you should take seriously the claims and promise of Christianity" is one thing; to say "I think you're irrational and pitiable for not doing so" is quite another. Thus the person of no professed faith who has a sense of Pascal's reasoning—or a pale imitation of it— may well be reluctant for a person of such views to be present with them.

Some kinds of **presence** are involuntary—determined by circumstance and shared hardship. The following comparison of two accounts of constructing the Burma railroad in the Second World War offers profound contrasts. On the one hand is a person of no professed faith and who could not allow anyone to be with him; on the other is a disciple who found transformative ways to be present and model **participation** with fellow sufferers.

In Richard Flanagan's novel *The Narrow Road to the Deep North* he portrays the complex character Dorrigo, fêted by the media for decades as a war hero, his public acclaim only matched by the narrow road of his inner numbness and self-loathing.[4] The heart of the book lies in the Burmese jungle in 1943, where Dorrigo is both the medical doctor and the senior officer among a band of a thousand prisoners being forced to work on the "narrow road" of the railroad, a project on which tens of thousands (one in three of those who were pressed into service) died. The men's lives are beset by starvation, cholera, and the sadistic violence of their prison guards. On countless occasions Dorrigo is asked by the Japanese camp commander how many of the men are fit to work. The truthful answer is always "None"—but that answer is unacceptable, so in the face of the commander's violent demands Dorrigo finds himself daily responsible for adding the least likely to die to those least sick—and thus for sending to hard labor men who can hardly stand with illness, injury, or hunger; a duty for which he feels guilty till his life's end.

Two hideous incidents sum up the novel. In one, the prisoner who sears Dorrigo's soul the deepest, Darky Gardiner, is brutally beaten to the point where he drowns in a sewage trench. Everyone is powerless, even the merciless guards doing the beating. In the other, Dorrigo attempts to perform an amputation of a leg with none of the requisite anesthetic instruments or staff to help him: the effort is pointless and indescribably agonizing, like the whole torture of imprisonment in the jungle.

4. Richard Flanagan, *The Narrow Road to the Deep North* (New York: Random House, 2013).

The experience is the making of Dorrigo—and the breaking of him. His testimony is set alongside three others. Most significantly there's his own life after the war, in which he becomes addicted to infidelity in a flawed attempt to reignite the dynamism of an emotionally evacuated existence, his constant, noble wife a symbol of the conventional life with which he can never again engage. Then there are the rag-tag soldiers who survived the enforced labor camps of Burma. "They died off quickly, strangely," the novel tells us, "in car crashes and suicides and creeping diseases." And then there's the ghastly camp commander himself, guilty of so many unspeakable crimes, who contrives to escape arrest yet over the subsequent decades acquires a dignity, not through repentance, but through destitution.

The lesson seems to be that the Burma railroad ripped the heart out of everyone who was there, those who died often horrible deaths, those who survived, those who ordered the deaths, and even those who became famous afterwards for their leadership and courage. The mockers surrounding Jesus as he hung on the cross said, "He saved others; he cannot save himself." It's an ironic summary of the whole gospel narrative. It's also a summary of the story of Dorrigo Evans, a man who survived the horror and made countless men's experience less ghastly than it would have been but lost his soul and self-respect in the process. He had truly been with the prisoners; but he could never allow anyone truly to be with him thereafter.

The Burma railroad must rival the concentration camps of Europe among the closest renderings of hell the twentieth century produced. War can be a terrible perversion and mutilation of many lives; but for some people it can have an intensity, meaning, and purpose they never know elsewhere. The horror can break many people; but it can make some, and inspire or reveal a depth of character that conventional life might never expose. Dorrigo didn't choose to enter the valley of the shadow of tortured death in Burma. He survived the war but lived for decades with a numb self-hatred amplified by the paradox of public acclaim. His story illuminates, rather more vividly than Pascal's account, the heroic character of a person of no professed faith, yet perhaps some of the potential flaws of unbelief, albeit in extreme circumstances. From a Christian perspective, Dorrigo's story is in many ways admirable but remains, as Pascal says, fundamentally sad: he's done great things but can't be with God, with others, or with himself.

A contrasting account, written from a position of faith, comes from Ernest Gordon, a twenty-four-year-old company commander in the 93rd Argyll and Sutherland Highlanders, who became a prisoner of war after the fall of Singapore in 1942. Like the fictional Dorrigo Evans he was pressed into labor on the Burma railway. Like Dorrigo it was a harrowing experience. But unlike Dorrigo, Ernest was to look back on those years as the crucible of his Christian faith.

The atrocity of the guards was similar. Men died by bayoneting, shooting, drowning, decapitating, or being worked beyond endurance. Some were tortured by having their heads crushed in a vice; others were buried alive in the ground. It was futile and soul-destroying. But for Ernest, a lot of the problems lay closer to home. It was such a struggle for survival, the prisoners were quite capable of being almost as cruel to one another as their captors were to them. But then, starting with small acts of kindness and thoughtfulness, emerged what Ernest Gordon came to call the *Miracle on the River Kwai*.[5]

It began with Angus. Angus started looking after one of his fellow soldiers, letting him have his own blanket. He would pass across his meal ration too. The soldier recovered.

5. Ernest Gordon, *Miracle on the River Kwai* (New York: Fount, 1995).

No one thought it could possibly happen. But Angus paid the price. He died from starvation and exhaustion. He'd laid down his life for his friend. One evening the guards counted the tools and found one shovel missing. The soldiers were assembled and told they would all die if no one owned up. The guard lifted his rifle to begin the slaughter. Straightaway a man stood up and said "I did it." The guard pummeled the prisoner with kicks and rifle butts until he was long dead. Finally the prisoners retrieved the body and marched back. Later that night a count was taken again: there'd been no missing shovel.

Ernest saw something extraordinary happening. "Death was still with us," he said, no doubt about that. "But we were slowly being freed from its destructive grip.... Selfishness, hatred, envy, jealousy, greed, self-indulgence, laziness and pride were all anti-life. Love, heroism, self-sacrifice, sympathy, mercy, integrity and creative faith, on the other hand, were the essence of life, turning mere existence into living in its truest sense.... True, there was hatred. But there was also love. There was death. But there was also life. God had not left us. [God] was with us." This was **glory**.

Ernest suffered pretty much everything the jungle could throw at him, including malnutrition, malaria, a tropical ulcer, and even the removal of his appendix. As a result he was put on the death ward. There he was on the receiving end of the gentle care of Dusty Miller, a gardener from Newcastle, and a Methodist; and Dinty Moore, a Scottish Roman Catholic. Their constant attention, their willingness each day to boil rags and wipe clean and massage Ernest's damaged legs, melted Ernest's agnostic heart and moved the spirits of many prisoners. He had met God. As he put it, "Faith thrives when there is no hope but God." Eventually Dusty and Dinty moved Ernest from the ward to their hut on higher ground, constructing a new bamboo addition for the purpose. One soldier sold his watch to buy the drugs needed to treat Ernest. To everyone's astonishment, Ernest started to recover.

This was the way not of clinging to life, guarding it, or preserving it, but of letting hates, fears, lusts, and prejudices die. As Ernest said, "We were beginning to understand that as there were no easy ways for God, so there were no easy ways for us. God, we saw, was honoring us by allowing us to share" in what it means to labor, the agony arising from loving the world so much. When finally the prison camp was liberated and the fear that the prisoners would be slaughtered by the Japanese proved unfounded, it was the prisoners themselves who persuaded the liberators not to exact retribution on the Japanese guards. Most of the officers in Ernest's section knelt down by the guards to give them water and food, to clean and bind up their wounds. "What fools you are!" an Allied officer called out. "Have you never heard the story of the Good Samaritan?" Ernest replied.

Ernest survived the war. He went on to become a Church of Scotland minister, and for many years he was Dean of the Chapel at Princeton University. In time, he discovered the truth about his companions: that two weeks before VJ Day a Japanese guard, exasperated by Dusty's calmness in the face of provocation, crucified him. Meanwhile Dinty, the Scot, was already dead: drowned when his unmarked prisoner-transport ship sank under friendly fire.

Ernest's life, and those of his colleagues, illustrates that regarding oneself simply as a victim is one's own choice. One can live in bitterness, resentment, and fear, replicating to others such horrors as those one has received oneself; or one can live in grace, mercy, gentleness, generosity, kindness, and sympathy. Dusty Miller was crucified by his captors; but died in faith, hope, and love. Dorrigo failed, in the end, despite his heroism, to be with God, with others, or with himself. Ernest, through learning to be with others, found all three.

Being with those of no professed faith in a voluntary context must be about presence suffused with **enjoyment**: not as a tactic (that wouldn't be enjoyment), but as a genuine desire to be with the person, not only for the person's flourishing (given that there's a sincerely held difference of view about where that flourishing lies), but also for one's own joy.

A presence suffused with enjoyment says, in word and in gesture, in kindness and in humor, in patience and in faithfulness, "I'm here because I want to learn from you. I'm here because I want to share with you. I'm not constantly going to direct the conversation to surface areas where we disagree; but neither am I going to change the subject when such themes naturally arise. I'm going to wonder about your life and your longings. I'm going to look fearlessly at your tender memories and your unresolved anxieties; and I'm going to be prepared to disclose mine to you in return. I don't imagine I have the answer to every question you might have; my faith gives me no superiority over you, no reason to judge you, no right to patronize you. I'm fascinated to know what you think when you gaze into the blue sky yonder, the wide sea afar, the depths of your own soul and mine. I'd be interested in how your obituary would read if you wrote it yourself, what you'd like the next generation to remember about you, where you find peace. But I'd also like to sit beside you in silence and watch a sunset together, allow an aria to float amid our senses, attend to the ticking of a clock and the passing of time. In these and many other ways we'd allow our acknowledged difference to take away the assumption of intimacy or the distress at disagreement and discover how something new and nameless could grow, based not on projected consensus but on provocative and generative tension—yet tension within trust. In faith there's enough light for those who want to believe and enough shadows to blind those who don't. Deep down I've assumed you're in the shadows; but maybe you think the same about me. Let's find wisdom in the shadows and walk together to where we can perceive light."

Notice what such an approach does and doesn't do. It does assume a natural curiosity from both parties. It does trust that the Holy Spirit is working in the relationship, whether or not the moment ever arises when the person of no professed faith becomes a seeker, let alone a disciple. It does assume that both parties have a lot to learn from one another. It does relish the differences between the two parties and anticipate that these differences will prove a source of creative, rather than destructive, tension and a spring of energy rather than a drain of trust.

It doesn't presume that the default of no professed faith is a stable, probably permanent resting place. It doesn't shy away from difficult subjects or rely on stealth alone to communicate grace and truth. It doesn't stake all on a particular predetermined outcome of the relationship. While it does believe the most interesting thing about people is where they stand before God, it doesn't assume a third party can ever fully know the reality of such standing. It doesn't think there's any formulaic way in which such relationships come about or are conducted: if it's not *sui generis* and pursued for its own sake, it's not truly enjoyment.

There's no enjoyment without **attention**. Attention identifies the uniqueness that yields delight and enjoyment. While I believe Pascal is right about the inexplicability of unbelief, the way Pascal proceeds from his insight lacks grace—which, in this sense, is synonymous with attention and delight.

Attention avoids superficial judgments, hasty generalizations, and sweeping observations. It sets aside almost everything that has been learned in previous such relationships and is willing to begin with a clean slate. It is always expecting to discover something that it hasn't unearthed before. While attention may find settled unbelief hard to fathom, for the reasons Pascal advances, it doesn't assume any pathology lies behind it; and, while it may perceive in such unbelief a cause for sadness, even lament, it doesn't suppose that's the way the person actually sees it. While it may believe the most interesting thing about people is where they stand before God, it allows a person to describe, or otherwise disclose, what he or she believes is the most important thing about his or her character or identity. What attention invariably seeks are traces of what later come to seem a coherent story. What is the sequence of events, reactions, intentions, and outcomes that has led to this person dwelling in this space right now? What is the most charitable reading of the story and, should an alternative interpretation readily present itself, would it be welcome or helpful to mention and outline such a minority reading? Can the listener surprise the speaker by paying closer attention to the narrative than the speaker does and recalling details that the speaker had overlooked? Where might one discern the Holy Spirit to be at work, even without the speaker's realizing it?

The truth is that "those of no professed faith" names no common characteristics, tendencies, commitments, or convictions. Attention says, "I'm not terribly interested in what you don't believe. Tell me what you do believe." It pays close regard to diversity, particularity, uniqueness, idiosyncrasy. Much of this is what Pascal called "custom." Custom names the way habit, tradition, culture, and circumstance generate wisdom that comes as close as could be to what many people would acknowledge as faith. If that doesn't coincide with the life of the church, it may be because of difference of conviction; but it may just as easily be through lack of mutual acquaintance, understanding, respect, or common tribe. Attention dismantles the impulse to define oneself by what one is against and offers time and interest to elicit what one is wholeheartedly in favor of.

If there's one thing the person of no professed faith is unlikely to anticipate receiving from the disciple, it's **delight**. That's not just because disciples may gain a reputation for being earnest; more seriously, it's because they may evoke an expectation that they will be censorious. One can hardly say it's an expectation without good grounds. Leaving aside any superiority complex or tendency to be judgmental, such a censorious attitude to those of no professed faith arises from two mistakes. First, a confusion between the lapsed and those of no professed faith: it makes no sense to assume adherence to Christian standards by those who've never subscribed to Christian convictions. It's been the business of this chapter to elucidate the differences between these two kinds of people. Second, an incorrect understanding of what it means to be lapsed: as we explored in the first chapter, being lapsed is at least as likely to be connected to the shortcomings of the church as of the former disciple, and to chastise from the outset risks adding prejudice and ignorance to lack of grace and poverty of empathy.

But delight is the element of surprise that changes everything. It is genuine, spontaneous joy on the part of the disciple: and it is likely to evoke a dumbfounded, but deeply grateful, sense of affirmation from the disciple's companion. The most obvious moments of delight are the sheer shared joy of being a human being fully alive. But just as thrilling are the very particular characteristics and narratives—sometimes meeting social norms, sometimes not—that make up the true texture of human existence: the things one doesn't tell many people, the quiet hobbies, latent skills, talents yearning to find an outlet, loves longing to find a name. "I thought you'd be shocked; I expected you to say we couldn't be friends anymore; I wondered if you'd think it was a sin; I didn't realize people like you approved of this kind of thing": such are the admissions that anticipate rejection and condemnation, exclusion and humiliation. But an answer that screams gladness, that hoots with happiness, that embraces with understanding, that cries with the overcoming of prejudice and fear—such is the priceless affirmation that issues from sincere and spontaneous delight; this is the famous stone that turneth all to gold.

One might have expected this chapter to begin with **partnership**, because perhaps the most common way of being with those of no professed faith (leaving aside cold-calling evangelism with the intent to convert on the spot) is to identify them as "all people of good will" and seek to make common cause amid one project or another together. But I have deliberately left partnership to the end. It's not that these ventures aren't invariably worthwhile both as enterprises in themselves and as exercises that build trust and understanding among participants. Sometimes, as with broad-based organizing, they make a virtue of diversity and harness the different gifts and perspectives of each constituent part. Other times, as with conventional politics and commercial endeavors, dissimilar views on ultimate subjects are set aside to achieve more tangible, achievable collective goals. This is how society functions and often flourishes.

The weakness with partnership is the flipside of its strength: precisely because it has such potential to enable people to forget their differences and work on making positive change together, partnership can become a subtle way of avoiding being with the person who's different from oneself. Working with precludes the need to be with. Talk of proximate goals obscures the need to talk about ultimate purposes. It's a parable of the way society operates—for good and ill. Being with, as we have seen, doesn't avoid or bypass difference, but sees difference as the point of creativity and dynamism.

An inspiring model of partnership in this spirit is offered in the 2011 film The Intouchables.[6] Set in Paris, it portrays Driss,

6. The Intouchables, directed by Olivier Nakache and Éric Toledano, Gaumont/Weinstein 2011.

an immigrant from Senegal, living on either side of the law, who meets Philippe, an eccentric millionaire rendered quadriplegic after a paragliding accident. The chemistry between the two strikes up immediately, and it rests on Driss's ability to see him without pity, without shame, and simply with humanity, mischief, and disarming unsentimentality. Driss's job is to be a live-in caregiver: but quickly he becomes friend, confidante, and coach, as constantly conventional roles in regard to race, class, and disability are either reversed or given fresh context and value. Both men are, initially, untouchable: Driss, despite his talents, looks, and youth, because of his race, criminal record, unstable family, immigrant status, reckless habits; Philippe, despite his artistic and musical expertise, wealth, luxurious apartments, connections, because of his tragic condition, profound discomforts, and short temper that make him so hard to help. In a defining scene, Philippe takes Driss to the mountains to witness the glory of paragliding. Driss is horrified when it becomes clear that he must himself don the flying gear and sail through the skies; Philippe is just as taken aback when Driss makes it obvious that he sees being quadriplegic as no obstacle to Philippe's resuming his paragliding career. Each man enables the other to cross the boundaries of the unthinkable: they can see their own limitations, but not one another's. The film ends with glimpses of hope: Driss becomes newly empowered to be a stable and strengthening presence in the life of his family, while Philippe finds the courage to go on a long-anticipated date with an admirer from Dunkirk.

The point is not that the film, based on a true story, is perfect: it doesn't avoid all stereotypes in the process of subverting some. Nonetheless it offers a vivid portrayal of partnership that exposes both the vulnerabilities and the assets of both parties, and doesn't fundamentally presuppose that one party should become more and more like the other. If one sees the film as an analogy of a relationship between a disciple and a person of no professed faith, the challenge becomes more evident. Does the Christian identify with the quadriplegic Philippe, once a charismatic and compelling presence in society, now reduced to a limited, isolated existence—or with the playful but unsettled Driss, with no domestic stability, no belonging elsewhere, living on his wits with mixed success? The analogy pushes the disciple to set aside anxiety about controlling or dictating the terms of the encounter, having the humility to realize how much there is to learn, how trapped one may be without acknowledging it, and how the person who initially seems a stranger and a threat may turn out to be a gift—and an angel.

One feels a constant impulse to turn the relationship into working with, to seek tangible outcomes, or even working for—in which Driss makes Philippe's life "better" by doing everything for him or Philippe gives Driss the money to "rescue" him from his disadvantaged banlieu existence. But the ability of the two men to be with one another is what the film is really about. There are ancillary blessings and achievements along the way, but if being with is the essence of existence—if evangelism is a means toward the end of being with, rather than vice versa—the two men find it not through one another, but in one another. Likewise, when being with a person of no professed faith, the disciple isn't perceiving the relationship as a mechanism for introducing the stranger to being with God and others; the disciple is anticipating this being an end in itself—perhaps their own truest experience of genuine being with. Thus what Driss and Philippe find—not through each other's unanticipated help, but in being with one another like no one has been with either of them before—is a parable of salvation.

CHAPTER 4

Being with Those of Other Faiths

When Christians speak of faith they generally mean three distinct, but not separate, things. First of all they mean a tradition of historical events, centered on the presence of God the Holy Trinity among us in Jesus Christ, the centripetal force *in* whom all the promises of Israel found their yes, and the centrifugal force *from* whom the Holy Spirit carried the good news to all the world. That good news was that through the incarnation God had shown the resolve never to be except to be for us and with us in Christ. In his passion and death Christ had shown there was no dimension of human life he was not prepared to reach and no depth of human sin he was not committed to redeem. In Christ's resurrection God had shown that sin, death, and the devil had no abiding hold on our lives or imaginations and that the end of all things was life with God, creation restored. In the sending of the Spirit and the empowering of the church, God had given us access to the three aspects of salvation Christ had made forever possible: forgiveness, healing, and eternal life. The presence of those things named, more than anything else, the living presence of Christ in the world. That is, more or less, what is often called the deposit of Christian faith.

If faith first means the past, it second means the future. Faith means a confidence that the new creation that God has promised will be a living reality in which all that has been rejected or downtrodden will be woven back into the design, that all discordant notes will be blended into a rich harmony, that there will be a banquet at which all may come to eat as God's companions. In particular it means that death is not the end of hope, but that beyond the dying of our light God will remake each one of us as a heavenly body out of all that is in us in this life that has turned to that greater light. In the meantime, faith names a certain notion of providence that, often despite the appearance of failure, suffering, and betrayal, trusts that all things work together for good if one lives in the rhythm of God's good time.

Secure in the heritage of historic events and the destiny of future promises, faith means to the ordinary Christian, third, a mode of living: abiding in the present. Ephesians 6 refers to the shield of faith. A shield doesn't stop bad things happening, it doesn't prevent you being attacked, it doesn't usually change the external reality that much. But it keeps your heart pumping and your life going and your spirits vigorous even when the slings and arrows of favor and fortune would otherwise destroy you. The present tense of faith means the grace to live without the need to have secrets about the past (because sins are forgiven) or fears about the future (because eternal life is promised). Faith is the freedom to be fully alive outside the prison of the past or the dungeon of the future. It is not effort expended but energy released, not an achievement to be grasped but a gift to be received. It exists definitively as infectious joy.

When Christians imagine and discover what it means to have faith alongside people of other faiths, all three meanings need to be borne in mind. So, for example, a common concern for Christians is whether those whose faith is not shaped around what God has done in Christ can be saved. This sounds initially like it's a conversation about the first kind of faith, the historical events, but in fact it's really a conversation about the second kind of faith, the future promises. The trouble is, no amount of millennial speculation or rapturous research can avoid the fact that Christian faith in the future, while full of conviction, is imprecise in its details. Christians become very exercised on the questions of who gets to heaven and how Christ's atoning work gets them there but tend to fall silent on the specifics of what heaven is actually like. There are two difficulties in the tendency to focus interfaith questions in this future dimension of faith. First, one can become embarrassed when pushed to articulate parts of the faith that have never been made fully explicit; second, one can seem ungenerous in being so certain that no one but people like oneself can find salvation, and this lack of grace seems to stand in contradiction to what I described earlier as the present dimension of faith, a life characterized by generosity and joy.

To take an alternative example, other Christians tend to focus on this third (present-tense) dimension of faith, whether conceived of as generosity and joy or as justice and liberation. This often evokes an uncritical eagerness to regard one kind of joy or liberation as being as good as another and a tendency to see the first dimension of faith, the historical tradition, as a burden and an encumbrance rather than an identity-forming gift. So Christians can face a corresponding pair of difficulties in their inclination to focus interfaith questions in this present dimension of faith. First, one can seem to treat eternal salvation as a device that can simply be secured through goodwill, appearing not so much to stress the universality of Christ's saving work as to deny the necessity of his atoning death; and second, one can seem so eager to be inclusive and to elide the specifics of historical traditions that one's articulations of faith can lose their moorings in the historical dimension of faith almost altogether. The perpetual call to leave our differences aside and go and do service projects together is commendable to the extent that the service projects are beneficial to the recipients and that it is easier to make relationships while doing something worthwhile. But it risks the conclusion that service projects alone are what faith is fundamentally about—a suspicion to which an overemphasis on faith in the present could easily give rise. Interfaith service projects have a great deal to commend them, but such projects should be an expression of faith and an opportunity for creative conversations around practice and tradition, rather than a substitute for faith.

It is for these reasons that, in contrast to one tendency to be overdetermined by the *future* dimension of faith and another inclination to be overcharacterized by the *present* dimension of faith, interfaith dialogue should, for Christians, be rooted in the first, historical, dimension as described above. The Christian faith is an existential and pragmatic reality and a dynamic anticipation of an inbreaking future. But before it is those things it is a tradition passed from the saints to the present day and recorded definitively in the scriptures. Only that historical tradition offers guidance in relation to the potential self-deceptions of the present and the potential false hopes of the future. It is with that heritage and specifically with those scriptures that interfaith dialogue should not necessarily end, but certainly begin.

Being with those of other faiths occupies a different place in the imagination of many disciples from that of most of the other forms of being with addressed in this book. Most refer to individuals or collectives that are themselves Christian, that Christians are already among, or that Christians are acutely aware of their calling to meet or serve. But many Christians call few if any people of other faiths friends, have only a small number of such people in their professional or personal circle, and are confused about whether such people should be regarded as those to whom they should witness or those whose difference should be tolerated and respected. Even when Christians are present with those of other faiths, that presence is perhaps more often than not the result of neighborliness or collaboration on a third-party-generated agenda rather than a genuine desire to know and know more about their conversation partners. Thus a discussion of being with those of other faiths can't start in the usual place, with presence. It must start with mystery and subsequently with attention; without these, presence might not happen intentionally, or even at all.

The theologian Paul Griffiths speaks acutely of why Christians so seldom write commentaries on sacred books of other faith traditions. He says, "We think we know what we'll find [there], and so we're disinclined to look closely. Theological conservatives tend to think they'll find a tissue of error and idolatry, and so they don't look at particulars. Theological liberals tend to think that they'll find lots of what Christians already know—which is true and good, of course—and so they don't bother to look, either."[1] For this reason being with those of other faiths needs to begin not with presence but with **mystery**—something that goes beyond thinking: "We know what we'll find there."

Three aspects of the mystery of those of other faiths must be stated at the outset. The first is that Judaism is not an "other faith." Why the Jews do not worship Jesus as the expected Messiah and the second person of the Trinity is a mystery and not a problem. Simply to say Jesus was rejected

1. Paul Griffiths, "Seeking Egyptian Gold: A Fundamental Metaphor for the Christian Intellectual Life in a Religiously Diverse Age," *The Cresset* 63, no. 7 (2000): 5–16.

because of the people's sin is not a sufficient answer. Neither is it enough to observe that Christian treatment of Jews in most of the subsequent centuries has given Jews no reason to respect, let alone be drawn to, the church. Likewise the place of Jews in God's purposes today is a mystery and not a problem. St. Paul wrestles with it in Romans 9–11. If it's a problem, the church feels it must solve it. But the church cannot solve it. The church must inhabit it with Jews, not solve it for them or for itself. Judaism is not, from a Christian perspective, a separate religion from Christianity: its God is the same God, its prayers are directed to the same place, its traditions shaped the practices of the church, one of its children is the person Christians call their savior.

The way the church prays with the Jews is a significant indicator of what the church thinks it is. It is a prayer of thanksgiving, certainly, for the people who, through Abraham and Moses, bore the covenant that Christians understand as being embodied in Jesus; a prayer of confession, undoubtedly, for centuries of persecution and estrangement from the people on whom God's seal had been set; of praise, surely, since the psalms, the hymnbook of Israel, remains the hymnbook of the church; and only then, after the previous three, of intercession, that the ancient division be healed and that the two sides come better to appreciate what their counterpart holds so dear. As an image of mystery, perhaps the Transfiguration, where Moses and Elijah stand on either side of Jesus like Israel and the church, may model a way to think about the relationship.

The second aspect is that if Judaism is the parent of Christianity, Islam is its cousin. The wonder of Islam is its simplicity and its practicality. It seeks to dismantle the elaborations of Christianity, its sacraments, priests, liturgies, and endless accretions—of which it sees Jesus as the epitome—which get in the way of a direct address between God and the believer.

At the same time it's about making a sustainable society, and it is very concerned about those things that threaten such a society, including notably violent clashes, business relations, and intoxicating substances. Its simplicity and pragmatism come together in the notion of submission. Thus it engages the directness and intensity that draws people to Protestantism and the everyday adaptability and universality that draws people to Catholicism. Islam isn't, as it is so often portrayed in the era of Islamist terrorist threats, fundamentally foreign and other to Christianity; it's a close blood relation, with similar features and vital insights to offer.

The third aspect takes us to Hinduism, Buddhism, Sikhism, Jainism, and Zoroastrianism, in particular, and less widespread faith traditions, more generally, for which there is a poignant question: how can it be that people sincerely hold to convictions and practices and devotions that contrast in greater or lesser ways with the faith of the church? When Peter says to Jesus, "Lord, to whom [else] can we go? You have the words of eternal life" (John 6:68), he speaks for the whole church in its bewilderment that anyone could seek salvation elsewhere. The church cannot hope to be with these other traditions in the same way as it seeks to be reconciled with the Jews. But it can still be with them in the sense of being present and attentive to them, and finding delight, since there is no greater way of enriching one's own faith than being exposed to a very different tradition that forces one to name and appreciate and better express the key elements in one's own. There is also significant opportunity to participate and partner with other traditions, particularly in the area of civil society where a church and a mosque or gurudwara or temple may, for example, work together to address issues of violence or community division in a troubled neighborhood or to tell the story of multicultural flourishing to celebrate a local anniversary.

To pray with a person of such a different tradition is always to risk turning the difference of the traditions from a mystery into a problem. Christianity and Buddhism are not divided: they were never one. A Buddhist may say that the secret is to discover that suffering is not real, while a Christian may believe that the secret is to discover that God is in the midst of suffering and that we are never closer to God than at such moments and thus that suffering is more real than anything else. It is pointless trying to reconcile such differences, and shared prayer risks trivializing them. To sit in silence together is perhaps the best way to be with a person of another tradition: this is being with God and seeking, but not assuming the terms of, being with the other. One can pray for other traditions, but it is much better to do so having shared presence, given attention, taken delight, and been with in participation and partnership. Thus does prayer both motivate and arise from being with.

To be captivated by the mystery of another faith is like learning a new language or discovering a new country. Ancient Greek doesn't have an ablative case. Indonesia is a land dominated by the ubiquity and proximity of the sea. Ireland is deeply ambivalent about what ought to be regarded as its border. The Inuit have dozens of different words for snow. Such information opens the doors of a mystery, makes one question the certainty that lies behind habitual words like "everyone" and "normal," and invites one, proverbially, to walk a mile in another person's shoes. It's not so much about gasping at the exotic; it's more about reexamining one's own tradition to disentangle the familiar from the true.

Particularly unhelpful—precisely because it is a way of treating those of other faiths as a problem rather than a mystery—is the widely invoked threefold distinction between exclusivist, inclusivist, and pluralist views. Exclusivists quote Jesus's words in John 14:6, "I am the way, the truth and the life. No one comes to the Father except through me," and take them to mean that Christianity represents the only true religion. Other religions may express some truths, but only Christianity embodies *the* truth. Inclusivists are inclined to believe the saving work of Christ can apply to adherents of other faiths, particularly ones whose lives have been lives of integrity and truth-seeking. Inclusivism is associated with Karl Rahner's term "anonymous Christian," given to those who seem to represent quasi-Christian ideals within other faith traditions. Pluralists assume that all the major religions provide equally valid paths to salvation. No one tradition is superior to any other: each has sacred rituals, holy people, and a commitment to love God and one another.

This tripartite formula is unhelpful because it shrinks the nature of faith to a pursuit of individual existence beyond death—rendering of little account the great history of the respective traditions and the precise activities in which these convictions have issued. It is a classic case of using faith rather than enjoying it—of seeing God as fundamentally a means to an end. It assumes as normative what I earlier called the second or future dimension of faith, and, while it makes reference to the third or present dimension, it is largely silent about the first dimension, the heritage of tradition. And yet, as I have already suggested, it is this first dimension that is the bedrock of Christian identity. Without it, Christianity is bound to seem like an assortment of arbitrary and culture-dependent conventions concerning mutual well-being and eternal survival. If one looks in any detail into the specific and in some cases historically grounded convictions in different religious traditions, focusing on personal salvation quickly becomes absurd, because different traditions have profoundly differing notions of the nature of the human condition from which persons are to be saved, profoundly differing perceptions of the God who is taken to be doing the saving and of the divine action that constitutes the saving, and profoundly differing visions of the blessed state that constitutes the result of that saving action or process. Focusing narrowly on personal salvation distorts other faiths and at the same time offers an impoverished account of Christianity, which is much more than simply a mechanism for achieving postmortem survival. Jesus ceases to be the overflowing of God's love and becomes a first-century vigilante on an undercover operation to get a bunch of souls out of earth before sundown. Providence ceases to be the rolling down of God's righteousness like a never-failing stream and becomes a complex forensic equation of how many souls can be squeezed into heaven with the aid of the four spiritual laws. When trying to understand Christianity, at least as much as other faiths, personal salvation is not the place to begin—or end.

Beneath this urge to commend such a typology lies a sociological or philosophical desire to designate some sphere of human action or conviction as religion. It's not clear that Christianity has any particular stake in being regarded as one among a broader genus called "religions," nor that it should self-consciously engage in a beauty parade in which it presents itself as the best in such a genus. I'm broadly agnostic on the question of whether there's such a generic thing as religion that Buddhists and Christians have in common. I'm inclined to be suspicious because I sense that to accept that Buddhists and Christians are both part of a more overarching area of human culture called "religion" risks subscribing to a self-definition that renders both of them irrelevant. Religion, in this sense, generally means a set of behaviors, moral norms, and practices that connect individuals and groups with some sense of security about life beyond death. Again, the emphasis is generally on the second and to a lesser extent the third dimension of faith described earlier. The irreducible distinctiveness of Christianity lies, however, primarily in the first dimension, the historical tradition. But in order to conform to a general definition of religion, each faith tradition is always likely to be asked to elide the parts of its identity that are unique.

The subtle agenda here is that religion becomes an aspect of culture that by definition has no purchase on any kind of truth that has an existential bearing on political reality. The state deals with matters of the mind and the body, and religious people deal with matters of the soul (if it even exists). If one takes a diverse set of campus ministers at an American university, one could, only half-jokingly, say that they're all liberal Protestants really. That's not some kind of "anonymous Presbyterian" doctrinal claim; it's the naming of a tacit acceptance that, if they want access to the university's resources and meeting space and goodwill, they have to accept at least in practice a set of liberal Protestant assumptions—that faith is primarily an articulation of inner dispositions and feelings, that it's best to be sheepish (at least publicly) about making converts, that it's terrific to put a lot of energy into service projects, and that no one has any stake in constituting a significant ideological challenge to the campus or national political status quo. Tick all those boxes and you get to be called a religious group. The fact that incarnational Christianity, for example, makes almost diametrically opposite claims about the body, suffering, and death to the claims and understandings upheld by most forms of Buddhism ends up being neither here nor there. To suggest that these faith traditions are two diverse manifestations of a fundamentally unitary phenomenon is to bend those traditions out of recognizable shape for some purpose that's not designed to serve either. One may speculate that concern about other faiths has tended to arise in Christianity not from a humble desire to learn, understand, and discover, but from anxiety about identity and convictions that had seldom previously been in question but now were exposed to intriguing alternatives.

To describe constructively how Christians might approach the mystery of other faiths, we may consider the story of the two women in 1 Kings 3:16–27.

> Two women who were prostitutes came to the king and stood before him. The one woman said, "Please, my lord, this woman and I live in the same house; and I gave birth while she was in the house. Then on the third day after I gave birth, this woman also gave birth. We were together; there was no one else with us in the house, only the two of us were in the house. Then this woman's son died in the night, because she lay on him. She got up in the middle of the night and took my son from beside me while your servant slept. She laid him at her breast, and laid her dead son at my breast. When I rose in the morning to nurse my son, I saw that he was dead; but when I looked at him closely in the morning, clearly it was not the son I had borne." But the other woman said, "No, the living son is mine, and the dead son is yours." The first said, "No, the dead son is yours, and the living son is mine." So they argued before the king.... So the king said, "Bring me a sword," and they brought a sword before the king. The king said, "Divide the living boy in two; then give half to the one, and half to the other." But the woman whose son was alive said to the king—because compassion for her son burned within her—"Please, my lord, give her the living boy; certainly do not kill him!" The other said, "It shall be neither mine nor yours; divide it." Then the king responded: "Give the first woman the living boy; do not kill him. She is his mother."

It's hard to imagine anything that could be dearer to oneself than one's own newborn child. Solomon perceives that the true mother would rather part with the child than see it die, because love is expressed in mercy more than in a brutal form of justice. But is not faith as dear to the believer as one's own dearest relative? Is that not what baptism means—that one is engrafted into Jesus in such a way that one cannot imagine being separated from Jesus any more than one could imagine consenting in the death of one's child?

Christians do not approach those of other faiths seeking hybrid or eclectic faith. Eclectic faith being like the woman in the story who said, "It shall be neither mine nor yours; divide it." How could one imagine creating a hybrid faith made out of choice highlights from the world's religions? Is such a cocktail not a sign that, like this second woman in the story, one is not truly inscribed into any one of them? This story nudges, provokes, stretches the imagination to perceive that it would be better, from a Christian perspective, that someone be a wholehearted follower of a faith other than Christianity than that they pursue no faith or that they strive to mix a cocktail of whatever tastes good with ice and a slice of lemon. The precious details of the origins of Christian convictions are not ones that Christians are in a position to give away or divide or barter over. It's quite possible to imagine discussing the quality of a religious experience or the implications of a social commitment in a way that is deeply appreciative and admiring of another faith tradition: but the heritage of faith is more like the baby. One can't take a sword to the heritage of Israel, the transformation in Jesus, and the emergence of the church in the power of the Spirit and somehow hope to emerge with the best bits. This is the lesson of the story from I Kings: if an undue effort is made to affirm the convictions of both women, the baby dies. Only when there is a risk of the faith of Jesus Christ being removed in favor of a generic claim of "everybody is right" does the genuine cry of faith shout up.

Christians don't talk with people of other faiths because there's a common core, named faith, religion, humanity, civilization, or consciousness that they all share. On such a view the more we talk with one another, the closer we get to the one thing we are all searching for. But if faith is not, for Christians, the end of searching but the lost sheep's acceptance of being found, this motivation is based on a false description.

What, then, is another faith in Christian eyes, if there is no basic thing called "faith" or "religion" from which to generalize and if it is better to be a sincere adherent of another tradition than an eclectic consumer of several?

These words from Matthew's Gospel suggest where other faiths belong in Christian theology.

> In the time of King Herod, after Jesus was born in Bethlehem of Judea, wise men from the East came to Jerusalem, asking, "Where is the child who has been born king of the Jews? For we observed his star at its rising, and have come to pay him homage." When King Herod heard this, he was frightened, and all Jerusalem with him; and calling together all the chief priests and scribes of the people, he inquired of them where the Messiah was to be born. They told him, "In Bethlehem of Judea; for so it has been written by the prophet: 'And you, Bethlehem, in the land of Judah, are by no means least among the rulers of Judah; for from you shall come a ruler who is to shepherd my people Israel.'" (Matt. 2:1–6)

The wise men are one of the most vivid portrayals in the New Testament of honest seekers after truth coming from beyond the faith of God's children. People of integrity come a long way—a very long way—using the best scientific and devotional materials available to them. That journey from the East characterizes a Christian perception of what it might mean for non-Christians to make a sincere search for truth. But crucially these sages make their way to *Jerusalem*. In Jerusalem they are exposed to the historical deposit of faith constituted by God's revelation to Israel. Through exposure to that unique and unsubstitutable revelation, they discover that the Messiah is to be born in Bethlehem. Here is a pattern to guide Christians' perceptions of both science and other faiths. Wisdom can get people to Jerusalem—in other words, can in some sense get a sense of what is meant by the God of Israel; but only revelation can get them to Bethlehem—to the God of Jesus Christ, made known as a tiny, vulnerable, needy baby. Research, study, prayer, meditation, discipline, searching, science can get you to Jerusalem; but only revelation can get you to Bethlehem. Bethlehem, with its vulnerable God in human flesh and its anticipation, in the magi's gifts, of his future suffering, is an emblem of what is unique about Christianity.

The heart of the Christian faith is not, in this sense, in Jerusalem. The heart of the Christian faith is in Bethlehem. Christians have little or no stake in arguing that there is a God, unless that claim is accompanied by witness that this is a God whose life is shaped never to be except to be with us in Christ. And the shape of that witness comes in the manger at Bethlehem. What saves us, in Christian terms, is not that *any* person went to the cross; it is that *this* person, this man born without a home, soon a refugee, raised among humble Jewish folk, *this* person went to the cross. That is what Bethlehem represents. Arguments for the existence of God and generalizations about religion tell us none of that.

So Christians applaud and welcome ways in which other faiths help chart a path to Jerusalem. But they do not mistake Jerusalem for Bethlehem. In this sense it is hard, in the context of being with those of other faiths, to talk about **glory**. Glory is not a generic thing that many traditions can find or disclose in what I have called Jerusalem. It is a specific thing that is found through Bethlehem. It is the discovery that, in John Betjeman's words, "The Maker of the stars and sea / Become a Child on earth for me"—that, in a simple liturgical sense, "God was Man in Palestine / And lives to-day in Bread and Wine."[2] God has the power and the will to bring people of other faiths into the glory; how this is done remains a mystery, and one that can't be rendered or resolved by appeals to democratic right or basic justice. That those of other faiths may find the glory is not a conviction or a demand—it is a prayer. The best way to support that prayer is, as always, through witness and example.

Turning from mystery and glory to **enjoyment**, there is a further insight to be gleaned from the conclusion of the burning bush story, where God is telling Moses how the people will be delivered. God says, "I will bring this people into such favor with the Egyptians that, when you go, you will not go empty-handed; each woman shall ask her neighbor and any woman living in the neighbor's house for jewelry of silver and of gold, and clothing, and you shall put them on your sons and on your daughters; and so you shall plunder the Egyptians" (Exod. 3:21–22).

Paul Griffiths describes the significance of this passage for how Christians are to be with people of other faiths. He says this treasure is indeed treasure. But the Egyptians do not know how best to put it to use. The wisdom of God guides the Israelites and they alone perceive that the purpose of the Egyptian gold is to be turned into objects that worship God. The dangerous dimension of this is that the same gold that can ornament the glorification of God can also be turned to the creation of idols. The philosophy of the pagans or the wis-

2. John Betjeman, "Christmas," in *Collected Poems* (Cambridge, MA: Riverside, 1959), 177–79.

dom of non-Christian traditions can likewise be turned into idolatry; but that is not its purpose. Its purpose is to glorify God, and thus it is something that Christians lack and need. Thus "the gold of the Egyptians is precious, desirable, to be sought with eagerness. We are therefore motivated to grapple with, to probe, to explore, and to ingest, the particulars of the religiously alien in all their alien specificity, because it is precisely in those specificities that we will find—if we can find—the precious things we seek, even though we don't know as we seek them just what they are or what we'll do with them when we've found them."[3]

Thus Christians are to enjoy people of other faiths and in doing so to discern which parts of those other traditions should be put to use enriching and adding wisdom to the Christian faith and which parts should not be put to use, but treated with suspicion as potentially idolatrous. Enjoyment is a single word that expresses what Griffiths calls "to grapple with, to probe, to explore, and to ingest." To assume a priori that every aspect of another faith is idolatrous is simply to neglect the way God brings gifts through the agency of the stranger. But to assume that every aspect of another faith is straightforwardly transferable or seamlessly analogous or easily adaptable to Christian practice is simply not to be paying **attention**.

An appetite for mystery and enjoyment needs to issue in detailed attention. Paying attention to Christianity itself yields a deeper, and apparently more modest, motivation for being with non-Christian believers. It is simply for people to be profoundly enriched by the gifts that come from the stranger. Christians enter the conversation expecting to be given gifts. What Christians learn in their tradition is that they depend first of all on God and secondarily on the com-

3. Griffiths, "Seeking Egyptian Gold."

93

munity of faith; but they also depend on the stranger. Here are some examples that are drawn from the heritage of Christian faith.

Israel showed its faithfulness to God in its openness not only to the orphan and the widow—but also to the alien. The Old Testament is a litany of testimony to the way the stranger brings unexpected gifts to the people of God. Melchizedek brings out bread and wine and offers a blessing to Abraham, and thus he becomes a kind of archetypal member of another faith like the wise men in Matthew. Pharaoh is the foreigner who feeds Jacob's family through the famine. Balaam offers Israel a blessing in the sight of her enemies. The Moabite Ruth epitomizes the faith and faithfulness of the stranger. Achish of Gath hides David when he is being pursued by Saul. The Queen of Sheba is the world's recognition of the wisdom and wonder of Solomon. Cyrus the Persian opens the way for the Jews to return from exile. In the book of Esther, Ahasuerus, another Persian, saves the Jews from the genocide plotted by the menacing Haman. Israel's story cannot be told without such people of other traditions and cultures of faith. Meanwhile, when the genealogy of Jesus comes to be written, names like the non-Israelite Rahab and Ruth are indelibly inscribed within it.

Central to the reception of Jesus's proclamation of the kingdom are a series of foreigners who understand it better than those to whom the gospel is first proclaimed. Jesus says of the centurion whose servant he is asked to heal, "Not even in Israel have I found such faith." Jesus heals ten lepers, but it's only the Samaritan who turns back to thank him and praise God. It's the Syrophoenician woman who insists that if Jesus can feed the Jews and have many baskets of crumbs left over, there must be crumbs enough to feed the Gentiles. The Roman soldier Cornelius is the one whose visit from an angel pushes the church into revising its understanding of Gentile faith. And it's in the figure of a Samaritan that Jesus tells his followers that they should see the model of a good neighbor.

Thus there never has been a Christianity that is not dependent on the stranger—particularly the stranger of a different faith tradition—for wisdom, example, revelatory moments, or even its very survival. Being with those of other faiths is not the convergence on a consensus. It is the opportunity for Christians to receive unexpected gifts from strangers as their forebears have done so many times before them.

This is the best context in which to talk about **delight**. God exalts the humble and humbles the exalted. Christians who believe they have it all are right, provided they recall with humility that they only have so long as they are prepared to receive, whether the one with something to give be the threatening Cyrus or the despised Samaritan. The people of Nazareth could not believe the well-known carpenter's son could be the Son of God. The early disciples could not believe the hostile Saul could be the charismatic apostle Paul. In just the same way it can be very hard for Christians today to accept the curious people through whom God chooses to be made known and to act and the surprising place where God chooses for the infant Jesus to be recognized first by humble social outcasts. But recognition of a pattern turns dismay into delight: it is a matter of grace that the Holy Spirit blows as it chooses; and a matter of wonder and joy that the failures of the church do not limit God's ability or will to redeem humankind or usher the kingdom through human agency. The trick is to turn that delight in God's grace into genuine relishing of the difference and discovery to be encountered in being with the religiously other.

Paying attention means approaching **partnership** with a healthy energy but a degree of caution. Partnership is more about working with than being with. It highlights and celebrates different qualities respective to each agent and how together they can be more than the sum of their parts. Christians can bring healthy energy to partnership with those of other faiths. There are indeed many things they can achieve together that they could not do alone. To assist Sudan, a Muslim agency is much better placed; to aid South Sudan, a Christian one. To achieve urban regeneration or reconciliation in Bradford or Leicester requires faith groups from several traditions to work together so that no single approach seems to be setting the agenda or assuming the right to chair the meeting. More subtly, there are times when the Christian notion of forgiveness needs to be central; there are other times when the Muslim idea of obedience may offer more immediate social outcomes.

So why the need for caution? Because partnership can disguise ways in which government agencies can seek to implement policies through so-called faith-based organizations, offering money, influence, and prestige in return for political capital. Such strategies can instrumentalize congregations and reduce them to the utility of their grassroots links and local knowledge. Relating to each other as good neighbors has many good aspects; but it is always liable to lapse into using rather than enjoying one another and combining to solve problems rather than encountering to apprehend mysteries. It turns face-to-face engagement into side-by-side endeavor. Underlying this broad tendency is the abiding temptation to revert to the invariably worthy and attractively achievable goals of working with in order to displace anxiety or reluctance toward the less tangible and more challenging demands of being with. As ever, working with can be a gentle and less threatening introduction to being with; the two can often coincide creatively and generatively; the point is never to let it become a substitute.

I have left presence and participation till last. As I said at the beginning, Christians can't simply rely on habits of neighborliness or the circumstance of physical proximity to inscribe the practice of **presence** among those of other faiths. More often they have to choose to do it. I am suggesting they choose to do it because they desire to be best placed to receive gifts from strangers. These gifts are of broadly three kinds. The *scrutiny* of strangers pushes Christians to identify, clarify, articulate, and refine their own traditions, convictions, and hopes. The *faith* of strangers challenges Christians' imagination, practice, and truth-claims and offers opportunities to discover wisdom and insight in unexpected places. The *company* of strangers creates occasions for Christians to receive blessing from the generosity, dignity, courage, and humility disclosed when the Holy Spirit chooses to grow fruits whose provenance Christians haven't already prejudged.

Being present to other faiths isn't dialogue between one -ism and another; it is encounter between one people and another, one person and another, one Christian, one Muslim, one Hindu. The first step in dialogue is to establish what it means to be present to one another. It is natural for Christians to propose that the form of being present be sharing a meal together, since it is at the heart of Christian experience that Christ is made known in the breaking of bread. Sharing food discloses significant dimensions of many faith traditions and provides a suitable opportunity for the beginning of interfaith conversations, since food is so close to perceptions about the source and destiny of life. Being with those of other faiths requires people to set aside time simply to be present to one another with no agenda beyond that which makes it easier to be present; for Christians this rests on a conviction that God's divinity is made present in our humanity. It's best to be with a small enough group that each may know one another's names after the first meeting and expect to become close acquaintances after several meetings.

The simplest way to be with one another, to **participate**, is to read sacred texts together. This may be done in more than one way. A text may be introduced by a representative of the tradition from which that text comes and taken as an entry-point into a description of the whole tradition. Several texts may be set alongside one another from different traditions around a common theme, such as ecology. Or each member of the group may together study a single text that derives from one tradition as if it were a sacred text from their own tradition. Such discipline and attention evoke questioning, insight, conflict, and discovery of one's own tradition as well as that of others. On occasion it may be appropriate to do a simpler version of this in public: for example to invite speakers from each of the major global faith traditions to address an issue such as the environmental crisis from within their own tradition before a live audience. This is a way of encouraging the sprouting of further dialogue groups as well as demonstrating the fruits of such dialogue in insight and good will.

Another kind of participation is journeying together. Journeying together is a physical and metaphorical notion. If a group of people can journey together physically, they can gain a better understanding of one another and the destination to which they are headed. Christians see this in Moses's guiding his people through the wilderness, through Jesus and the disciples' journey to Jerusalem and Paul's journey to Rome. A physical journey together to the local mosque or to Varanasi on the River Ganges is a perfect way to embody the spirit of humble engagement Christians seek to display in interfaith dialogue. But just as significant is the metaphorical journey that emerges from a personal history of engagement in settled and in trying times, of joint statements in troubled seasons and reasoned disagreements on matters of significance, that together accumulate a common awareness that these have been conversations that have really mattered.

Why do such things? For the world, perhaps, because there is nothing the world needs more than examples of how to sustain reasoned disagreement over issues that evoke passionate expressions among people who have no foundational starting points to fall back on. For people of other faiths, possibly, because the Christianity that emerges in generous-hearted dialogue with strangers is offering others what as Christians we believe are the words of eternal life. For the salvation of souls, also, since the joy of forgiveness and eternal life is such that Christians cannot keep from singing, and to love the stranger is to long for that stranger to know the source and destiny of all love.

But genuinely to be with the person of another faith means to say, "I'm doing this for me. I am a person in need. I am a person who would like to learn better how to pray, how to live a disciplined life, how to fast, how to meditate, how to be a gracious presence in the life of my neighbor. And I represent a tradition that needs to learn how to bring people of different races together, how to hold diverse opinion within one body, how to break our addiction to violence, how to use power to set people free. These are things I personally and the tradition I represent have to learn. I'm learning to be with those of other faiths because I believe that God shows me things through people like these. And what I say to them is, 'Thank you for being messengers of God to one another and to me.'"

CHAPTER 5

Being with the Hostile

E arlier (in chapter 1) we explored those who'd experienced rejection by the church and whose distance was significantly of the church's own making. In *Incarnational Ministry* we considered those who'd made mistakes and needed to come to terms with them and those who were hurt and were looking, over time, to be reconciled with one another. Here we look at another context altogether: those whom the church has not set out to oppose, but whose hearts are nonetheless set against Christians to the extent that they may be described as hostile.

We may think of four degrees—anger, antagonism, agitation, and aggression. (1) Some people feel genuine anger toward the church or Christians, perhaps resentful of the church's social influence or hold on people's imaginations, determined to rid the world of guilt, negativity, or prejudice about some minority groups (for example over treatment of LGBTQ people), or inclined to see religion in general as the source of all the world's problems. (2) Sometimes this can issue in genuine antagonism, either directed at individuals or aired in public settings, perhaps with strong language, and moved to clear articulation that Christians are a problem and constitute a group that society would be better without. (3) Seldom in the West, but more often in contexts where Christians are very much a minority, there can be actual agitation, either toward legislative and legal strictures that prevent Christians having open access to opportunity and resources, or in the direction of social discrimination that makes them more and more marginal. (4) More extreme forms of hostility can issue in aggression and physical violence, endangering property, livelihood, well-being, and even life itself. International terrorism is the most discussed form of such threats, but in some nations outright hostility between social groups on the grounds of religion is endemic.

Such hostility was common in the experience of the early church. "They will put you out of the synagogues. Indeed, an hour is coming when those who kill you will think that by doing so they are offering worship to God" (John 16:2). "We are afflicted in every way, but not crushed; perplexed, but not driven to despair; persecuted, but not forsaken; struck down, but not destroyed; always carrying in the body the death of Jesus, so that the life of Jesus may also be made visible in our bodies. For while we live, we are always being given up to death for Jesus' sake, so that the life of Jesus may be made visible in our mortal flesh" (2 Cor. 4:8-11). "See, I am sending you out like sheep into the midst of wolves; so be wise as serpents and innocent as doves. Beware of them, for they will hand you over to councils and flog you in their synagogues; and you will be dragged before governors and kings because of me, as a testimony to them and the Gentiles. When they hand you over, do not worry about how you are to speak or what you are to say; for what you are to say will be given to you at that time; for it is not you who speak, but the Spirit of your Father speaking through you" (Matt. 10:16-20).

The centuries before Constantine are littered with accounts of Christian martyrs. Polycarp, Bishop of Smyrna, was burned at the stake in 155 CE and, when the fire did not consume him, was run through with a dagger for refusing to renounce the faith. His exchange with the proconsul is vivid:

> The proconsul then said to him, I have wild beasts at hand; to these will I cast you, unless you repent. But he answered, Call them then, for we are not accustomed to repent of what is good in order to adopt that which is evil; and it is well for me to be changed from what is evil to what is righteous. But again the proconsul said to him, I will cause you to be consumed by fire, seeing you despise the wild beasts, if you will not repent. But Polycarp said, You threaten me with fire which burns for an hour, and after a little is extinguished, but are ignorant of the fire of the coming judgment and of eternal punishment, reserved for the ungodly. But why do you tarry? Bring forth what you will.[1]

Perpetua, a twenty-two-year-old noblewoman, and her slave Felicity were martyred in Carthage in 203 CE in honor of the emperor's birthday. After many persecutions they were eventually taken to the arena where they were attacked before the crowd by animals before being killed by gladiators— Perpetua having to assist the gladiator to put the sword to her throat, he being so nervous that he could not do it unaided.[2] What's common to these two and many other such accounts is that martyrdom did not take place in a vacuum; the prisoners had extensive interaction with their persecutors, time to

1. Alexander Roberts and James Donaldson, trans., *The Martyrdom of Polycarp*. http://www.newadvent.org/fathers/0102.htm.

2. Herbert J. Thurston, SJ, and Donald Attwater, eds., *Butler's Lives of the Saints*, 493–98, https://archive.org/stream/ButlersLivesOfTheSaints CompleteEdition#page/n524/mode/1up.

be present with and attentive to them—and thus exercise at least some dimensions of being with.

Martyrdom is by no means an exotic practice restricted to classical times. Above the west door of Westminster Abbey in London are statues of ten twentieth-century martyrs: Maximilian Kolbe, Manche Masemola, Janani Luwum, Grand Duchess Elizabeth of Russia, Martin Luther King Jr., Óscar Romero, Dietrich Bonhoeffer, Esther John, Lucian Tapiedi, and Wang Zhiming. Undoubtedly most martyrs die in obscurity.

Most obvious, yet often overlooked, is the fact that Christianity is founded on a story of persecution. Jesus knew hostility from the beginning of his life and ministry. "When Herod saw that he had been tricked by the wise men, he was infuriated, and he sent and killed all the children in and around Bethlehem who were two years old or under, according to the time that he had learned from the wise men" (Matt. 2:16); "The Pharisees went out and immediately conspired with the Herodians against him, how to destroy him" (Mark 3:6). When Jesus tells the disciples how to respond to hostility, he's offering not just an ethic, but a prophecy. "Love your enemies, do good to those who hate you, bless those who curse you, pray for those who abuse you. If anyone strikes you on the cheek, offer the other also; and from anyone who takes away your coat do not withhold even your shirt. Give to everyone who begs from you; and if anyone takes away your goods, do not ask for them again" (Luke 6:27b–30). Jesus offers seven categories of enemy: those who hate you, curse you, abuse you, strike you, rob you, demand things from you and steal from you. In this list Jesus predicts what he himself is about to undergo. Jesus went to the cross because he loved his enemies. As he went to the cross he was hated, he was cursed, he was abused, he was struck, he was stripped of his clothes and humiliated. And yet at every step he responded not with hatred but with love.

Thus the Gospels are extended accounts of how God models being with the hostile in Christ. Being with is the goal, but it is also the method of bringing order, stability, and peace.

Nonetheless the hostile names the most challenging of all contexts for being with. This isn't because addressing hostility lends itself naturally to working for or working with in a way that might make being with seem inadequate or somehow passive. It's because no method of interaction seems likely to bring about the softening of relations that constitutes the only preliminary to the parties becoming any kind of a blessing to one another. I have often been critical of the practice of being for, citing its tendencies to avoid face-to-face relationship and to assume that something must be done but it's for others to do the doing. Yet there is perhaps no more appropriate context for being for than that in which being with—let alone working for or working with—seems impossible.

Contexts of hostility defy generalization, so in this chapter, rather than take an overarching approach, I shall offer particular examples and reflect on what they illustrate and demonstrate about the practice of being with. While extreme situations might seem unhelpful to the extent they are untypical, they do offer the hope that if being with is possible in a desperate situation, perhaps it's possible anywhere.

In Terry Waite we find a man confronted by the challenge not just of hostility but of isolation. While involved in negotiating the release of hostages in the Middle East, he was betrayed by his captors and himself incarcerated. He dwelt in an underground cell for five years, chained hand and foot to the wall and blindfolded when anyone else was present. He was utterly alone and isolated from the world and was allowed no reading material. One night the chains were unlocked and he was commanded to stand up. He was taken to another room to lie down and face interrogation. His captors assumed he was a CIA agent. When the desired answers were not forthcoming one of them put a pillow over his face and sat on it. His feet were struck many times with a wire rope. He had to be helped back to his cell. Yet he did not give in to bitterness: "As I sat in the dark, I do not remember feeling anger against my tormentors. Rather, I felt pity. Pity that anyone could be so cowardly as to treat a helpless individual in the way I had been treated."

But there was more to come. A few weeks later one of the lead captors told Waite he had five hours to live. It was time to prepare for the worst. Again, Waite had resources to draw upon: "I remembered something I had read, I think in the writings of the late Carl Jung, the Swiss psychotherapist. He said that when one faces the extremities of life, allow your body to come to your aid and it will. Now, at this critical point, I understood what he meant for I lay down on the floor and fell asleep." When the five hours were up he was led into another room and commanded to stand. His throat was dry as he contemplated not death, but pain—the pain of the bullet he was anticipating any second. Asked if he wanted anything, he requested to write a letter to his family and another to his friends. Only one was permitted, scratched while peering under the blindfold. He was given one further concession and he said the Lord's Prayer out loud. "Then I was told to turn around and I felt cold metal against my temple. It stayed there for several moments before it was removed and I was told: 'Another time.'" Thereafter he faced a further four years of incarceration, but there was no more torture because the captors now believed his story about who he was.

Waite speaks vividly about what he and other hostages discover: "a strength within themselves they never knew they had." This is what emerges:

They learn, as I did, to live for the day and not to allow themselves to think far ahead. They learn to control imagination and discipline their thoughts so they are not reduced to quivering wrecks every time a key turns in the door. The experience is very difficult and there are times when one experiences terror. Of that there is no doubt. The most terrible uncertainties and agonies are felt by friends and relatives who wait on the outside, not for one moment understanding what the person they care for is undergoing.

Waite remains under no illusions about the misery and cowardliness of hostage-taking. But his faith in human nature led him to the conviction that "suffering, while always difficult, need not destroy. Out of the most dreadful circumstances it is possible for unexpected creativity to emerge." And not just creativity, but solidarity also. On visiting the mother of a hostage beheaded in Iraq many years after his own release, Waite heard her speak of her terrible loss, but also of her insight: "my suffering is little different from the suffering of a mother in Iraq who has lost her child as a result of warfare."[3]

Waite's account details the isolation, fear, pain, suffering, and horror of his captivity and the duplicity, betrayal, manipulation, ignorance, cruelty, and cowardice of his captors. There is no suggestion that the captors were open to his being with them: this is not a story of how Paul and Silas, through God's grace and their own generosity, move the heart of their jailer to bring about his conversion (Acts 16:25–34). There's also an

3. Terry Waite, "Inside the Mind of a Prisoner," *The Mail on Sunday*, August 24, 2014. http://www.dailymail.co.uk/news/article-2732940/In side-mind-prisoner-hostage-negotiator-held-five-years-Beirut-Hooded -beaten-given-five-hours-live-hostage-horror-TERRY-WAITE.html. For an extended account see Terry Waite, *Taken on Trust* (London: Coronet, 1994).

ambivalence about whether the hostility arises because he is a Christian. He goes to Lebanon in his role as the Archbishop of Canterbury's Special Envoy to mediate and negotiate for the release of hostages; but it seems his captors assume he's working for the CIA. In time they realize he's not; but it still takes several more years for him to be released. Ambiguity abounds. Nonetheless, Waite's story offers significant lessons in being with. He does not succumb to anger; instead, he feels pity. He learns and remembers the habits of being with himself. He is comfortable and at peace in being with God. He is realistic about the little he can do to be with others beyond the situation—but active in doing what little he can, in writing a deathbed message to his wife and friends. He is hopeful that "suffering, while always difficult, need not destroy." And he draws enough compassion and sympathy from his own experience to be empowered to be with another—in this case Ken Bigley's mother—in hers, and elicit from her wisdom that only the attention of being with can yield.

It's important to take stock of what Waite's testimony does and doesn't reveal about being with the hostile. **Presence** is costly: presence as a mediator made Waite vulnerable to being taken captive (a fact for which Waite was much criticized by those who saw him as a maverick do-gooder). **Attention**, to the captors and their inscrutable ways, is vital, not least for one's own survival; and when in solitary confinement is one's only source of "with," however undesirable. **Mystery** is everywhere—how one human being can do this to another, how people can be filled with such single-minded hatred, how distant relatives and friends can imagine what is going on, how God can be present even here. **Delight** is next to impossible, except in flashes when one realizes the preciousness of life, even a life as attenuated as this one is, and perhaps in very modest doses through quirky ironies and rueful reflections. **Participation** is explicitly precluded through

solitary confinement. **Partnership** is likewise impossible if
all relationship other than hostility is withheld. **Enjoyment**
is, however, evident. This is the best way to describe what
Waite develops as a way of being with himself. His ability
to control his imagination and discipline his thoughts are
forms of truly enjoying—and thereby training—himself; but
there is no opportunity to enjoy his captors. (Ken Bigley's
mother, however, does find a way—one that verges creatively
on being for.) And it's not entirely inappropriate to speak of
glory—not perhaps within the situation, but in his being
given grace to survive it. Terry Waite's release was perhaps,
along with peace in Northern Ireland and bloodless transfer
of power in South Africa, the most prayed-for intercession
item in the Church of England in a generation. For a person
to emerge from such hell and be able to write with dignity,
wisdom, and grace afterwards—that must touch on **glory**.

Thus this account of being taken hostage has indicated
that attention and mystery are still areas of promise, enjoyment and presence are exceptionally demanding, delight and
glory are fragile, and participation and partnership almost
out of the question.

One context that blends elements of the second and third
scenarios outlined at the start of this chapter is the situation
of Christians in Pakistan. Christians number around 2.5 million in Pakistan, around 1.6 percent of the population. Around
half are Roman Catholic, half Protestant. Educated Christians
were prominent supporters of Jinnah's Muslim League prior
to independence in 1947, but Christians became more isolated
thereafter as most Hindus, Sikhs, and Zoroastrians migrated
to India. Minorities were officially protected after the country became an Islamic Republic in 1956, but laws and national
identity became increasingly focused on the Muslim majority.
Attitudes to Christians hardened in the 1980s and 90s, with
educational establishments becoming more intimidating

environments in which to be in the minority as Muhammad Zia-ul-Haq, President from 1978 to 1988, increased the profile of Islam in law, banking, and government. After 9/11 Christians came to be seen by many as representatives of the non-Islamic West—the invaders of Afghanistan and subsequently Iraq. Tension focused on blasphemy laws, by which protests made by Christians about their social situation started to be interpreted as insults to the Prophet Muhammad or desecration of the Qur'ān; severe punishments could result. Stories of forced conversion to Islam spread, along with various kinds of intimidation, harassment, and discrimination, with death threats becoming more common. Major suicide bomb attacks took place, killing 127 at All Saints, Peshawar, in 2013 and seventy-five at Gulshan-e-Iqbal Park, Lahore, on Easter Day, 2016.

One example of the sociology of hostility is the clearance of *katchi abadis*, or slums, in Islamabad, which has been defended on the grounds that most of them are inhabited by Christians. Such a view, in the eyes of one commentator, confirms the prejudice that "Christians as a group can never be conceived of as anything more than filthy outcasts unworthy of being given even the most rudimentary rights and protections afforded to 'real citizens.'"[4] It's hard not to read this clearance of areas where Christians live as giving institutional justification for vigilante attacks on individuals to which Christians are routinely subject. The term *chuhra*, often used to describe Christians, was originally the term given to a particular caste of Hindus from which most Pakistani Christians descend. Once the British started taking a census in the nineteenth century, previously fluid population groups gained fixed identities: this meant first that the so-called

4. Daniyal Yusaf, "The Tragedy of Being Christian in Pakistan," *Daily Times*, December 8, 2015. http://dailytimes.com.pk/opinion/08-Dec-15/the-tragedy-of-being-christian-in-pakistan.

chuhra group of landless people became regarded as untouchables; but second, that when, toward the end of the century, the opportunity to convert to Christianity arose, large numbers of *chuhras* took the chance to escape their lowly caste status and in the process gain access to education and health care. With the coming of the Islamic Republic, the historic caste associations resurfaced: jobs in waste management and inferior housekeeping roles have come to be set aside for *chuhras*, areas of cities have become ghettoes for them—both sanctuary and prison—and stereotypes abound, linking them with dirt, gambling, alcohol, and poverty, together with the perpetual accusation of blasphemy. Intolerance of the group is not so much religious as it is about the impulse toward social uniformity and the widespread disdain, even disgust, toward those considered inferior.

One helpful study surveys the responses of Christians to this pervasive culture of intimidation.[5] Many who have the means have sought to emigrate, sometimes claiming asylum in the UN camps of Thailand, Sri Lanka, or Malaysia. Those without this option have in some cases marched in protest, seeking to attract attention from national authorities or international bodies. In 1998, when Ayub Masih was handed the death sentence for blasphemy in Sahiwal, Bishop John Joseph, the Roman Catholic Bishop of Faisalabad, shot himself in front of the court in protest. Not all protests have been peaceful. When suicide bombers killed twenty people at two churches in Youhanabad, Lahore, in 2015, two Muslims suspected of being terrorists were lynched by the Christian crowd who mimicked pervasive features of Muslim attacks, such as chanting, in distressing ways. But the majority Chris-

5. Maqsood Kamil, "Religious Extremism and Christian Response in the Context of Pakistan," http://infemit.org/wp-content/uploads /2015/07/Kamil.pdf.

tian response has been to offer forgiveness. One study, conducted after the death of 127 worshipers at All Saints, Peshawar, in 2013 found that of 337 people interviewed, 308 spoke words of forgiveness such as the conviction that judgment is for God alone, that "they don't know what they are doing," prayers to God to show them mercy so that they may repent and be restored, and prayers "that they would know how precious life of a human is."[6] What has not happened is that people desert the church. Participation remains high and disciples' hold on faith is tenacious. But faith and forgiveness have not generated love or peace. Citing the work of Michael Nazir-Ali, himself raised in Pakistan, this study speaks of four kinds of potential dialogue: the dialogue of life, the dialogue of deeds, the dialogue of specialists, and the dialogue of the interior life.[7] (We could call these four spheres of being with.) But the survey offers this somber conclusion:

> When it comes to the dialogue of specialists, Christians suffer from lack of such specialists who can engage Muslim scholars. Christian leadership training institutions are largely responsible for such a dearth. None of the major theological institutions teaches courses on Islam or Christian-Muslim relations. Sadly, constitutionally, politically, socially and intellectually, Christians have no voice and no influence. They constantly look towards the western world to save them from these appalling and life threatening situations. However, in many cases it proves counterproductive.[8]

6. Matthew Jeong, "Report to the Diocese of Peshawar and All Donor Friends about Our Visit to 62 Victims of the Bomb Blasts on 22 April 2014," quoted in Kamil, "Religious Extremism," 18.

7. See Michael Nazir-Ali, *Mission and Dialogue: Proclaiming the Gospel Afresh in Every Age* (London: SPCK, 1995).

8. Kamil, "Religious Extremism," 20.

With Terry Waite we explored an extreme case of what it means to be with those who are determined to use you and have no interest in enjoying you. Here in the case of Pakistan is a study in what it means to be with a people from whom one cannot withdraw, but who for the most part have no desire for participation, no aspiration to partnership (for Christians to hold senior public office is against the law), who share no delight, and who seem to resent even presence. This is not the situation often presupposed by accounts of mission—where Christians hold present and historic privilege and power and have a majoritarian mindset (if not reality); quite the contrary, this is a beleaguered group jeopardized by legal, social, religious, and cultural oppression.

Attention abides, nonetheless. Attention seeks out those few who are prepared to see the rights of minorities, if not yet the blessings that can come from them. Attention sees nuances and makes distinctions that many would miss—for example between Sunni and Shi'a, recognizing that all in Pakistan who are not Sunni are in some form of predicament. Attention sees the difference between caste oppression and religious discrimination, and it seeks to disentangle the two. Attention seeks to understand what is honorable and just in the Sunni ideology, and it seeks to appeal to those standards rather than to what might be seen as Christian or Western ones.

Once again we see the severe limitations of being with when it comes to the hostile. But again those limitations are at least matched by those of working for (which is practically irrelevant in this case) or working with (which is no more possible than being with, perhaps less). Participation in and partnership with the global church are the best ways to build solidarity and hope to increase security. Insofar as the blood of the martyrs is the seed of the church, there is a glimpse of glory in the faithfulness of presence. But beyond that, attention—usually from the safest achievable distance of being for—is for the most part as far as incarnational mission can go.

The 2015 Charleston church shooting offers a rather different context of hostility. Emanuel African Methodist Episcopal Church, one of the oldest of all African American congregations and long active in civil rights advocacy, was gathered for worship. Nine people, including the senior pastor, Clementa C. Pinckney, were killed after the suspect, twenty-one-year-old Dylann Roof, joined them for an hour as they shared in Bible study, before opening fire. One account described how "the gunman specifically asked for the church's well-known pastor, the Rev. Clementa C. Pinckney, who was also a state senator, and sat next to him in the Bible study. First he listened, they said, then he argued, and eventually he began ranting against black people, until finally, he stood, drew a gun and fired, reloading as many as five times."[9] As he left he stood above an injured congregation member and spoke what was later described in court as "a racially inflammatory statement." The Federal Department of Justice decided to regard the attack as a hate crime and murder rather than terrorism.

Like Terry Waite's experience, accounts of the Emanuel Church shooting concern something that is, in its immediate impact (though not, of course, in its searing damage), over and done. But this shooting is an extreme case of a phenomenon that, like the situation in Pakistan, is endemic—a racial and cultural prejudice and hostility that adopt religious guise, or at least find places of worship easy targets for their

9. Nikita Stewart and Richard Pérez-Peña, "In Charleston, Raw Emotion at Hearing for Suspect in Church Shooting: Victims' Families Address Dylann Roof," *New York Times*, June 19, 2015. http://www.nytimes.com/2015/06/20/us/charleston-shooting-dylann-storm-roof.html?_r=0.

expressions of searing hatred. But unlike both the Terry Waite and the Pakistani church contexts, in this case the perpetrator is alive, visible, known, and named. How does one relate to a person who has demonstrated such hostility? Just a few days after the shooting several bereaved congregation members and relatives came face-to-face with the young man who had carried out the terrible act of violence and murder. As one account narrated it, "It was as if the Bible study had never ended as one after another, victims' family members offered lessons in forgiveness, testaments to a faith that is not compromised by violence or grief. They urged him to repent, confess his sins and turn to God."

Both on the night of the attack and even in the aftermath of the killings, the congregation was determined to be with Dylann Roof as best they knew how. "'We welcomed you Wednesday night in our Bible study with open arms,' said Felicia Sanders, the mother of twenty-six-year-old Tywanza Sanders, a poet who died after trying to save his aunt, who was also killed. 'You have killed some of the most beautiful-est people that I know,' she said in a quavering voice. 'Every fiber in my body hurts, and I will never be the same. Tywanza Sanders is my son, but Tywanza was my hero. Tywanza was my hero. But as we say in Bible study, we enjoyed you. But may God have mercy on you.'" For the themes of this study, this is the most poignant statement of all: "we enjoyed you." These words of witness, at once beautiful and tragic, identify precisely why and how this massacre was different from so many other grotesque moments in America's story of race and story with the gun. The congregation had truly been with a man who nonetheless resolved to take the lives of so many of their members.

Prior to being with the perpetrator, the community needed to be with one another. Being with oneself and being with God together (both considered in *Incarnational Ministry*) are not things that can be bypassed: in this most trying of circumstances, it's the community's strength in these two areas that speaks most eloquently. What this account shows is that the Emanuel Church congregation offered an exemplary form of interaction with the young man who nonetheless remained determined to exact havoc among them: they were present with him, attended to him, and, most remarkably, *enjoyed* him—as the account explicitly articulates. Possibilities for participation or partnership were offered, and the fact that the killer spent an hour sitting next to the pastor suggests they reached deep; but his heart was nonetheless set on murder.

A later account describes how attitudes broadened and deepened one year after the killings. Nadine Collier told Dylann Roof that she forgave him. He had taken from her something she valued very greatly. She realized that she would neither talk to nor hold her mother again. Yet she was able to balance judgement with mercy: "You hurt me. You hurt a lot of people. If God forgives you, I forgive you." She had no doubt this was honoring her mother's convictions. "I know she would have said, 'That's my baby. I taught her well.'" And she also learned that goodness is stronger than evil. "Forgiveness is power," she said, sitting in her North Charleston home. "It means you can fight everything and anything head on."[10]

To forgive a perpetrator is to allow that person to remain a part of your story—to abide with you. The impulse is often to try instead to forget (however absurd that might be in the circumstances of murder), but forgetting precludes forgiving

10. Bob Smietana, "A Year Later, Families of the Charleston Shooting Victims Still Wrestle with Forgiveness," *Washington Post*, June 17, 2016. https://www.washingtonpost.com/news/acts-of-faith/wp/2016/06/17/forgiving-dylann-roof-is-taking-a-heavy-toll-on-those-left-behind-but-theyre-not-giving-up/.

because it is a subtle impulse to avoid being with the person who has hurt you. Forgiving means facing the often excruciating work of allowing the destructive person to be with you in ways that no longer destroy. Thus the decision to be with—or, at least, to be for—is a decision not to give in to hatred. Mother-of-three Bethane Middleton-Brown found herself, after the killings, also raising the four children of her late sister, the Rev. DePayne Middleton Doctor. Though she took to calling Dylann Roof "Lucifer," she made a deliberate, conscious step not to let his hate infiltrate her mind. It's too soon to forgive, she believes—"the wound is still fresh"—but she wants to replicate her sister's overflowing love and faith.

Overcoming racism seems like an insuperable task. "All it takes is one bullet, or one piece of hate to kill someone." She can find herself overwhelmed with grief. But her convictions are buoyed up by grace. "God is taking me to a higher level," she said. "If the man who killed my sister was looking for hate—he came to the wrong place." Likewise Shirrene Goss seeks to tell a bigger story than the story of bitterness: to overcome the killer's hatred with God's love and her own love. Of her murdered younger brother Tywanza, she says, "He was a shining star. He had to shine brightly." But forgiveness itself doesn't come overnight. "I can't say that I have forgiven" Dylann Roof, she says, a year after the killings. "I know I need to as a believer." But she is nonetheless committed to respond to hatred with love. "Spread the love of Jesus. That's the simplest thing anyone can do." And answers will eventually come.

This second account, one year on, adds texture to the raw agony and dumbfounded disbelief of the very early encounter. Again, what speaks loudest is the community's ability to be with themselves and to be with God together. It's clear that their preparedness to be with the person who hated them so much and caused them so much pain is drawn from habits and dispositions learned in the practices of discipleship and ministry. There are hints of the transfiguration that exhibits glory: "God is taking me to a higher level." Amid the profound attention of grief, there is realism about the wider context that made an atrocity like this conceivable: "I don't know if we will ever be able to overcome racism"—these are words of one who has evidently pondered the possibilities in light of faith and is sober at the challenge they present.

Some might say that the Emanuel Church shootings were about race alone and not about religion. But they occurred in the midst of worship, after an hour of Bible study that the killer attended. This was hatred of people, a hatred that was violently expressed while those people were pursuing their Christian faith. And the survivors and families reacted in explicitly theological terms. Being with the attacker as he serves his sentence will be very difficult indeed; as the accounts show, forgiveness can be elusive and can by no means be rushed; but there are ways to be with short of forgiveness, and forgiveness is not a panacea that makes being with straightforward. As with the other contexts described, being with has few answers in the face of violent, incorrigible, wild hostility; but it seems that other approaches have fewer still.

CHAPTER 6

Being with Neighbors

The neighbor marks the crossover from the first part of the book, which concerns individuals in the world, to the second, which concerns persons seen collectively. In this chapter I want particularly to address the sense of being overwhelmed by need, and at the same time I want to point out that different approaches may be equally valid according to diverging circumstances.

Let us begin with a series of alternative contexts in which the notion of neighbor arises. You're at home, busy with something important to you, perhaps intensely private, and in any case not to be interrupted, and a person who lives nearby appears at the door, knocking, enquiring, demanding, intruding. Or there's great news, of the end of a war, or terrible news, of the assassination of a beloved leader, or an unprecedented event, like an earthquake in the home counties or a drastic flood nearby—and one way or another conventional demarcations and boundaries break down, and you speak to people you'd usually no more than nod to and feel common cause with those who'd previously been more or less strangers. Or again, you're sitting on a train. There's a distressing noise from further up the carriage. A person is holding her head and grimacing, clearly in terrible pain. Something's obviously very wrong and you've no idea what it is, but you feel you have to look, you're impelled to draw near, you have an urge to ask other passengers if they know what's happening or what any of you can do. Or here's one more. You're staying in a friend's house. You're coughing, and it won't stop. It's not a normal cough—you grasp that there's something badly wrong. Your cell phone can't get any reception, and you realize you need to find a landline. You can hear music in the flat upstairs. You think, "I've got to knock on that door."

I've scattered these scenarios by way of introduction because I want to break the word "neighbor" down into its different connotations. I've chosen four emotive examples because I want to highlight the disconnection between the benign term "neighbor" and the degree of anxiety evoked by the question, "Who is my neighbor?" There are broadly three inferences of the word "neighbor." The first is literal: it's the person next to you, usually permanently, in the sense of the one who lives next door, but also momentarily, as in the one who's with you in the elevator or beside you on the bus. The second is rather abstract: it's the sense of neighbor as generalized other, whom you have not chosen but rather, for a longer or shorter time, been given—the work colleague with the unconventional eating habits, the argumentative person in the grocery store, the disconcertingly attractive person sitting next to you in the movie theater; but more generally the vacant lot beside your house, the person you see walking with lots of plastic bags, talking to himself, and, at moments of paralyzed compassion, a whole nation in the midst of civil war, a town you see in a television story about a devastating hurricane, or Antarctica as it rapidly loses its icebergs. Most discourse about the word "neighbor" circles around either these literal or abstract conceptions.

But there's an emotional pull to the word "neighbor." This apparently harmless word evokes a profound, visceral, and primal reaction. "Neighbor" becomes a cipher for "impossible demand." We spend our whole lives trying to gain control, to have enough money, enough comfort, enough security, enough trust in the people around us that we won't be dragged off the rocky boat into the merciless waves. But that's precisely what the neighbor threatens to do: the neighbor is the person who, through intrusion, manipulation, limitless need, or infuriating invasion, presents us with impossible demands. And we're divided, our hearts are torn, by the self-preservation and self-assertion that says, "No, I've tried so hard, for so long, to get to a place of sufficiency: I'm not having this interloper drag me down into the abyss," and the guilt or compassion that says, "That's a human being, that's a person who deserves my respect and support, that could easily one day be me—that has, at another time, been me." And it's that torn, confused heart that represents the challenge of being a human person in an individualized society.

If we look more closely at what lies inside the tangible fear of impossible demand, what do we see? We've already noted the sense that I will lose something. It may be space; it might be freedom; it could be resources, security, safety, or, at the very least, time and emotional energy. That's the force of the word "demand." But there's also the word "impossible." That's a subtler anxiety. If I'm bringing skills, experience, networks, or expertise, I will still, almost inevitably, given the scale and complexity of the demand, fail; and if I'm simply bringing a willing heart and a humble hand (in other words, nothing more or less than myself) I just won't have what's required. Either way it keys into an underlying fear of emptying out with no replenishment, like a balance sheet hemorrhaging losses or a blood donor giving out more than anyone can afford to lose. Impossible, insatiable demand leads to the overarching sense that this will take more than I've got and the consequent lapse into burnout, failure, exhaustion, or depression. For many, the answer to the question "Who is my neighbor" becomes, "The one who promises to drown me in a boundary-less ocean of need."

Emma Jane Kirby's novel *The Optician of Lampedusa* epitomizes this notion of neighbor.[1] It offers a fictionalized account of the October 2013 disaster in which three hundred migrants, largely from Eritrea and Somalia, died. The nameless (and therefore universalizable) optician lives on the tiny island of Lampedusa (population 6,300), 127 miles south of Sicily and seventy miles from the coast of North Africa. (Lampedusa was the site of Pope Francis's first official visit outside Rome, when in July 2013 he prayed for migrants living and departed and upbraided their traffickers.) Out at sea with eight friends, the optician hears the cries of migrants in the water. Standing on the cabin roof, this is what he sees.

Bodies were flung like skittles across the sea's glassy surface, some bobbing precariously, some horizontal and horribly heavy.... Every time a wave collapsed, a black dot or head was revealed. The sea was littered with them.

... How, he thought, how do I save them all? He lowered his outstretched arm slowly. In the water, hands stretched despairingly upwards, clutching at air, reaching futilely towards him. He could see yellowing eyes staring wild and wide at him, frantic at the hope of salvation.

He glanced down at his friends on deck. Eight. There were eight of them and there were scores, no, hundreds of people in the water. And they had just one rubber ring.

Even before he jumped down from the cabin and back

1. Emma Jane Kirby, *The Optician of Lampedusa* (London: Penguin, 2016).

onto the deck, the optician had understood that he would have to choose who would live and who would die. (27–28)

Kirby's novel identifies precisely the sense of being over-whelmed by need—but also the rewards of doing what one can, and the sense of solidarity established with those with whom one can engage. The strongest sense, nonetheless, is that the optician represents Europe and those in the water embody an ocean of need.

In this chapter I recount two stories that address precisely this profound, visceral feeling. The stories don't refute this emotion, nor do they provide a precise alternative answer to our question. If they do give an answer, it's not precisely the same one. But together I believe they recast the question in a way that provides us with a different question, one perhaps easier to answer, and more empowering to respond to.

In his 2014 book *Just Mercy: A Story of Justice and Redemption*, Bryan Stevenson, founder and executive director of the Equal Justice Initiative in Montgomery, Alabama, and professor of law at New York University Law School, portrays the reality of being black in America.[2] Stevenson describes what has shaped the notion of race in the US. Slavery casts an indescribable shadow. But there's also the reign of terror that pervaded the South from the end of Reconstruction till the Second World War. African Americans hear the talk of the new experience of domestic terrorism after 9/11 and say, "We grew up with terrorism all the time. The police, the Klan, anybody who was white could terrorize you. We had to worry about bombings and lynchings, racial violence of all kinds." There were countless ways black people could offend a white person that might endanger their lives.

2. Bryan Stevenson, *Just Mercy: A Story of Justice and Redemption* (New York: Random House, 2014).

Stevenson notes how the modern death penalty was created as "an attempt to redirect the violent energies of lynching while assuring white southerners that black men would still pay the ultimate price" (299). Convict-leasing was a routine method of criminalizing former slaves by convicting them of absurd crimes so that they could be leased to commercial enterprises and effectively forced back into slavery. The successes of the civil rights movement haven't eradicated the legacy of the Jim Crow era of segregation. Stevenson describes how racial profiling works in practice: sitting alone, smartly dressed, in a courtroom, he himself could be told to get out and wait in the hallway until his lawyer arrived, until he politely informed the judge that he was indeed the lawyer. Mass incarceration fits this overall pattern. As Stevenson puts it, "The extreme overrepresentation of people of color, the disproportionate sentencing of racial minorities, the targeted prosecution of drug crimes in poor communities, the criminalization of new immigrants and undocumented people, the collateral consequences of voter disenfranchisement, and the barriers to re-entry can only be understood through the lens of our racial history" (301).

Stevenson describes how the prison population in the US has increased from 300,000 in the early seventies to 2.3 million today. The cost has increased even faster, from $6.9 billion in 1980 to $80 billion today. One in every three black males born in this century is expected to go to jail. A horrifying number of children are incarcerated in adult prisons in the only country in the world that sentences children to life imprisonment without parole. Over 50 percent of prisoners have a mental illness, and there are more than three times the number of people with a serious mental illness in prison than there are in hospitals (188). And within this system lies a litany of dreadful, damaging, and often deliberate mistakes and miscarriages of justice, together constituting a system that Stevenson describes as being "defined by error" (16).

The story that forms the backbone of Stevenson's account is that of Walter McMillan from Monroeville, Alabama. The deepest irony of the story is that Monroeville proudly identified itself as the setting for Harper Lee's 1960 novel, To Kill a Mockingbird, an account of a 1930s white lawyer who bravely defended an innocent black man. Not only had Walter McMillan himself never heard of the novel but the law enforcement officers and justice representatives of the town contrived in Walter's case to subvert every value portrayed in its narrative. Walter started his own pulpwood business that gave him some economic independence but attracted suspicion from those who believed undereducated black men should know their place. Once Walter's philandering habits extended to sleeping with a married white woman, he was in danger. When the beautiful young daughter of a respected local white family was murdered, and when after several months no one had been charged, the county sheriff embarked on an elaborate plan to frame Walter, gaining damaging testimony from people Walter had never met and overlooking the fact that Walter had spent the whole morning of the crime entertaining guests for a fish-fry at his home. Due to the seriousness of the charge, Walter was put on death row even before his trial, one of many illegal and transgressive actions brought to bear against him in the subsequent proceedings. Fifteen months after his arrest, an all-white jury, in the face of overwhelming evidence, pronounced Walter guilty, and after they had recommended life imprisonment the judge escalated it to a death sentence.

Bryan Stevenson's organization, the Equal Justice Initiative, has, since its foundation in 1994, saved 125 men from the death penalty. Stevenson tells the story of his struggle for justice through the setbacks and successes of the Walter

McMillan case. One evening Stevenson drove deep into the woods outside Monroeville to a trailer park and was greeted by well over thirty family members who knew Walter was an unstable husband but found their hearts broken and their standing in the community shattered by the manifest injustice of Walter's impending execution. The whole community was being victimized, and otherwise decent white officials were becoming locked in to a narrative of denial, deceit, and dishonesty.

Stevenson would see Walter about once a fortnight, and gradually they came to be friends. Walter, it became clear, was a kind, decent man with a generous nature. Stevenson not only enjoyed the friendship; he realized that gaining his client's trust was crucial to winning the case. As he puts it:

> A client's life often depends on his lawyer's ability to create a mitigation narrative that contextualizes his poor decisions or violent behavior. Uncovering things about someone's background that no one has previously discovered—things that might be hard to discuss but are critically important—requires trust. Getting someone to acknowledge he has been the victim of child sexual abuse, neglect, or abandonment won't happen without the kind of comfort that takes hours and multiple visits to develop. Talking about sports, TV, popular culture, or anything the client wants to discuss is absolutely appropriate to building a relationship that makes effective work possible.

This is a story of **attention** and **enjoyment**. Finally in 1993, through the tireless work of Bryan Stevenson, six years after his trial, and after repeated breakthroughs and devastating setbacks, Walter McMillan was cleared of the charge of murder and released from jail to a wife who could no longer bear to live with him and a community that felt every scar of what he had endured all those years on death row. Walter and Bryan talked almost daily on the phone as he made tentative steps to reenter life outside. Walter shared the true depths of the despair he'd experienced watching other prisoners go to their executions. Stevenson earned Walter some degree of compensation for the injustice he'd suffered, and Walter resumed work cutting timber. But one day Walter was struck by a stray branch that broke his neck. During his long recovery, for two months he lived with Stevenson in Montgomery, one hundred miles to the north. For a few years after that Stevenson would bring Walter to New York to take questions in his law class at the university. But in time the effects of the broken neck hastened the onset of dementia, and when Stevenson visited Walter in a care home, Walter felt like he was on death row for a second time.

As Bryan Stevenson looks back on his journey with Walter, which is simply the most poignant and time-consuming of scores of such cases, he asks himself, in a spirit of **mystery**, why he does what he does. Sitting in tears after putting the phone down on a man who was to be executed later that evening, Stevenson looks back on twenty-five years of struggle against inequality, abusive power, poverty, oppression, and injustice, and realizes he doesn't do what he does because it's required or necessary or important, or because he has no choice. He does it because he is broken, too. Exposure to all this hurt and evil has revealed his own brokenness. In the words of Thomas Merton, we are bodies of broken bones. Stevenson believes

> Being broken is what makes us human.... Our brokenness is the source of our common humanity, the basis for our shared search for comfort, meaning, and healing. Our shared vulnerability and imperfection nurtures and sustains our capacity for compassion.

We have a choice. We can embrace our humanness, which means embracing our broken natures and the compassion that remains our best hope for healing. Or we can deny our brokenness, forswear compassion, and, as a result, deny our own humanity. (289)

Stevenson perceives that "we've thrown away children, discarded the disabled, and sanctioned the imprisonment of the sick and the weak—not because they are a threat to public safety or beyond rehabilitation but because we think it makes us seem tough, less broken" (290). He recalls victims of violent attacks and relatives of the murdered, "and how we've pressured them to recycle their pain and anguish and give it back to the offenders we prosecute … how we've allowed our victimization to justify the victimization of others. We've submitted to the harsh instinct to crush those among us whose brokenness is most visible" (290). But so doing simply leaves us all broken. Stevenson recalls from his college days in Philadelphia an old minister who would throw his arms wide as the choir were about to begin, and say, "Make me to hear joy and gladness, that the bones which thou hast broken may rejoice." This is **glory**. Finally Stevenson realizes, "The power of just mercy is that it belongs to the undeserving. It's when mercy is least expected that it's most potent—strong enough to break the cycle of victimization and victimhood, retribution and suffering. It has the power to heal the psychic harm and injuries that lead to aggression and violence, abuse of power, mass incarceration" (294).

I turn now to a very different kind of story—a novel and not a memoir, by and about a woman and not a man, in England not America, about suffering but not so much about injustice, and with other, perhaps more significant, differences that I'll return to later. Jojo Moyes's novel *Me Before You* tells the story of Louisa Clark. Lou, 26, is devastated when she loses her job at the local café, where her outgoing nature perfectly fits the diverse clientele and makes her feel she has a vital role in the community.[3] Having few qualifications, she has little choice but to take the hardest local job to fill: she becomes caregiver to Will Traynor, age thirty-five, who she discovers was paralyzed when hit by a skidding motorcycle two years earlier.

The job starts badly. There's **presence**, but not in the form of genuine being with. She's eager to please, to make tea, to cheer him up, to tidy, to cook—whatever it takes to break into the steely gloom of his static negativity. In a pivotal scene, Will receives a visit from his girlfriend back at the time of the accident, Alicia, along with his old London colleague Rupert. It turns out the two friends are full of dread because they've come to tell Will they've got engaged. Mortified with guilt, Alicia, as she leaves, explains to Lou that she didn't simply abandon Will; she spent months trying to do things for him—but he wouldn't have it and she gave up. After Rupert and Alicia leave, Will maneuvers his wheelchair to the mantelpiece and uses his stick to sweep to the floor every photograph on display there—many of which are of him with Alicia. Lou spends hours trying to repair the photo frames and restore the pictures to their former glory. Will is furious. He says, "You wanted to fix what I did yesterday.... It would be nice, for once, if someone paid attention to what I wanted. Me smashing those photographs was not an accident.... I don't want to have those bloody pictures staring at me every time I'm stuck in my bed until someone comes and bloody well gets me out again." To which Lou, provoked, with cheeks aflame and with nothing to lose in the midst of her failure, responds, "You don't have to behave like an arse" (73–74).

3. Jojo Moyes, *Me Before You* (London: Penguin, 2012). Also a 2016 film.

This confrontation marks a turning point. Thenceforth Lou has more respect for letting Will have some space in his sadness, and Will begins to take Lou seriously as a person in her own right and not just an agent of his family's attempt to mollify him. Will even allows Lou to cut his unkempt hair and shave his disheveled beard, a visible indicator of his emergence from furious depression. It seems he will let her do some things for him, after all. Encouraged, at her sister's suggestion, Lou develops a bucket list of things she thinks will help Will engage with the simple joys of living. Her ambitions lead her to take Will and his physiotherapist to the races to enjoy watching and betting on the horses. It turns out to be a desperately unsuccessful expedition, as a mixture of wheelchair-unfriendly facilities, bad luck, and an obstinately miserable Will ruin any sense of adventure and turn it into an afternoon of torture. The day sums up the catalogue of failures and humiliations Lou endures as she tries to rescue Will from his condition—and from himself.

Three further events qualify Lou's sense of what she's trying to achieve. Her unemployed father gets a job working for Will's father, and she responds not with gratitude but with anger that Will has tried to improve her life by making her family less dependent on her income. This anger, she begins to realize, makes her more sympathetic to what Will feels like when everything is being done for him. Lou's relationship with her boyfriend becomes increasingly strained, partly because her thoughts are ever more focused on Will, but also because she finds her boyfriend, obsessed with his fitness regime, has no notion of how simply to be with her, which makes her reflect ruefully on whether she's been any more successful at learning genuinely to be with Will. When her boyfriend and Will finally meet, she's furious with her boyfriend for being able to relate to Will only in a way that gives advice on body-strengthening and being unable to see the person beyond the physical paralysis. The irony is that she's not been much different for most of her time in the job. Will, who likes to call her Clark, starts to question her about her reluctance to make more of her abilities, saying, "Your life's even duller than mine"—which leads her to divulge a sexual assault in her late adolescence that cursed her with such a catastrophic loss of confidence that she became in some ways as paralyzed as her patient. Genuine **partnership** begins to emerge out of the debris of failed working for assumptions.

When Will gets a visit from a lawyer, a little detective work leads Lou to discover that Will is putting his affairs in order because he's planning in just a few months to travel to Switzerland to be assisted to die. Lou realizes she's a tool: her employment is the result of a bargain between Will and his mother by which Will promised to delay his suicide by six months and his mother hired someone to cheer him up, hoping he'd change his mind. As Lou and Will become more fond of one another, she dreams up and executes the perfect plan. She takes Will on a once-in-a-lifetime exotic beachside holiday, hoping to deepen their relationship, inspire him with the beauty of living, and put out of his head all morbid thoughts of the Swiss clinic. It's beautiful because for the first time there's a glimpse of real **participation**. On their last night, planning to spend the dark hours with him and express their budding love, Lou stands on the brink of triumph when Will shatters her exultation, saying he still intends to travel to Switzerland shortly after their return from their island paradise. Despite her utter dismay, Will insists. He is defined by his chair. She can see past it; but he can't—or won't. This is his explanation:

"You never saw me before this thing. I loved my life, Clark. Really loved it. I loved my job, my travels, the things I was. I loved being a physical person. I liked riding my motorbike, hurling myself off buildings. I liked crushing people in business deals. I liked having sex. Lots of sex. I led a big life.

"... It's not a matter of not giving you a chance. I've watched you these six months becoming a whole different person, someone who is only just beginning to see her possibilities. You have no idea how happy that has made me.... I don't want you to be tied to me, to my hospital appointments, to the restrictions of my life.

"... I don't want to look at you every day, to see you naked,... and not be able to do what I want to do to you right now.... I can't be the kind of man who just ... accepts.

"... I need it to end here. No more chair. No more pneumonia. No more burning limbs. No more pain and tiredness and waking up every morning already wishing it was over. When we get back, I am still going to go to Switzerland. And if you do love me, Clark, as you say you do, the thing that would make me happier than anything is if you would come with me." (426–27)

Lou is shattered, and spends the journey home thinking, "Why is this not enough for you? Why am I not enough for you?" She longs to have more time and is dismayed that he didn't confide in her earlier. Her anger and hurt get the better of her and she refuses to see him in his last days, until a phone call from Will's mother in Switzerland begging her to come persuades her; and that trip to the Swiss bedside creates a poignant frame for the story. The novel began with a prologue in which Will and his then-girlfriend Alicia, deep under the duvet, doubtless exhausted from the best sex the world has ever seen, oversleep. That means Will needs to dress rapidly before he rushes out into the street to come face to face with the reckless motorbike that all but kills him. The novel ends in a very different bedroom with Will and a different girlfriend, one who has learned she can't give him what he most wants, but is nonetheless beside him to the last, as he faces a death of his own choosing.

The title *Me Before You* suggests a book about how people change from the person they were before they met each other and, to some extent, about how Will finds himself incapable of showing the selflessness toward Lou that she shows toward him. But the real story of the book is how Lou comes to discover, clumsily and painfully, what it really means to stand before Will. It means to realize that you can't fix someone else's life; you can't be a performing clown or party organizer that cheers other people up; and that a true relationship can't be based on one person's plenty and another person's lack. Will and Lou find a relationship only when they realize they're both paralyzed, and Lou gives Will what he really needs only when she sits beside his bed in Switzerland and stops trying to be the fairy godmother whose magic wand turns all to gold. Will's real problem isn't his quadriplegia; it's his fantasy of an eternal youth of perpetual energy, sensation, and consumption, a fantasy he's obdurately determined to hold on to even though Lou is clearly offering him something immeasurably more mature, sustainable, and relational.

I want now to set this story of Lou Clark and Will Traynor alongside the account of Bryan Stevenson and Walter McMillan in the context of what it means to be with a neighbor.

The biggest contrast between the two stories is that Bryan chooses to work on behalf of Walter. Walter makes the original contact, but by the time he does, Bryan has already been working for two years as a lawyer determined to get justice and release for prisoners on death row that have no reason to be there. Bryan has oriented his life in the direction of meeting someone like Walter. By contrast, Louisa Clark has, at the outset, no desire whatsoever to meet, let alone care for,

Will Traynor. The class issues are reversed—in Bryan's case, while from a humble background, he is a college-educated Harvard Law School graduate coming into the territory of struggling folk in southern Alabama; in Lou's case, she is an underachieving, ambitionless young working-class woman coming into the territory of a family that until two years before exuded effortless perfection, and whose affluence reduces her to feeling like an awkward intruder. The difference here is that Lou's neighborliness is literal—she simply has no choice but to find a way to connect with Will, surly, miserable, and rude as he is. Walter, by contrast, is Bryan's neighbor of choice, which is a different thing.

But there's a fascinating similarity. Earlier I suggested that what makes the word "neighbor" so terrifying is that it seems to open the door to impossible demand. What seems special about Bryan, besides his evident legal genius and relentless appetite for work, is that he apparently can live with what, to most of us, would be an indescribable level of demand. He details the countless people on death row, the limitless flaws and shameful faults in the American legal system, the endless line of wrongful convictions and stitched-up sentences. He relates the times he's been overcome by tears as the horror of execution or the fury of corruption sinks in. But he never seems to stop. What seems so different about Lou is that she's the girl next door; living in the shadow of her more talented sister, struggling to sustain her impoverished family, quite content with her colorless boyfriend, with no desire to leave town or go to college or see the world. But by the end of the story she's even more overwhelmed by one neighbor than Bryan is by scores. Leaving the romantic dimension to one side, the lesson seems to be that if you're fully committed to be with even one person in all their struggle and complexity, that commitment will overwhelm you quite as much as a commitment to be with everybody. It only takes one neighbor, and attention to that neighbor's true need, to search the deepest recesses of your soul.

And another apparent difference leads to a second stirring similarity. Bryan's highly qualified: he's got family experience of homicide, since his grandfather was murdered during a bungled burglary; he's been to college and trained at Harvard; and he has done serious time with the Southern Center for Human Rights, based in Atlanta, Georgia, before setting up his own non-profit in Montgomery, Alabama. He has become a professor at New York University. Lou is not remotely qualified. Our first meeting with her details what she does know—and it starts with the number of steps from the bus stop to home. Her ambition is fulfilled in working at the local café. When she works for the Traynors, it's clear that the physiotherapist does the heavy lifting in every sense: she's just there to make sure Will doesn't find a way to slit his wrists. When Lou does try to do something for Will, like take him to the races, it's generally a humiliating failure.

It seems Bryan and Lou are opposites. But they both make the same discovery. When Lou shares her point of real pain with Will, a genuine mutuality begins to arise where both begin to see how trapped they each are, and they begin to recognize how the other one is offering a key that could perhaps give them release. Likewise what Bryan discovers is that the real joys of his job lie in the kind of fellowship and reciprocity he establishes with Walter and the camaraderie he shares with Walter's wider family. By the end of his memoir the lessons he's learned are not about his triumphs and victories but about his own brokenness and the fact that there's something deeper than justice and that's mercy, because at the end of all the anger and hurt and discrimination and cruelty and humiliation, you have to find a way to go on living, and that, in the end, means showing mercy to those who scarcely for one moment deserve it. Just as Lou discovers that being a true neighbor to even one person opens a vast canyon of impossible demand, such that her neighborliness and that of Bryan Stevenson are of the same quality despite their many circumstantial differences, so all four of the people in question—Walter, Bryan, Lou, and Will—find respectively that their common humanity as neighbors lies in their brokenness.

The word "neighbor" is a rather antiquated term except in one context: seeking to live the parable of the Good Samaritan. Elsewhere I have suggested that the best exegesis of the parable is to understand that the Samaritan is Jesus. And this provides the key that releases the identity and potential of the neighbor. If we see ourselves as the neighbor, the world looks like it does to the optician of Lampedusa: an ocean of impossible demand. But if we see the neighbor as Jesus, our perspective is transformed and the neighbor becomes the one who is coming to give us gifts, wisdom, insight, blessing—in short, coming to save us. It is Jesus, rather than we, who regards the whole earth as a neighbor and doesn't turn away from us in the anger and hurt and discrimination and cruelty and humiliation we inflict or receive; who is our advocate when we walk through the valley of the shadow of death, whether by our own or another's folly; and who waits beside us by the bedside of our wrong choices and in the confusion of our clumsy forms of love.

Jojo Moyes's novel *Me Before You* might just as well be a theological story in which Will discovers Jesus is not the neighbor who fixes his problems or cheers him up but who abides with him in his heart of darkness and shapes his whole life so as never to let him go. And Bryan Stevenson's memoir *Just Mercy* might equally be a theological account of how we do not have a high priest who cannot meet us in our brokenness but one who is able to speak with us about sports, TV, popular culture, or anything that we want to discuss, and who weeps when we face punishment and knows sorrows just like our own. We have an advocate with the Father who is our neighbor in heaven and whose Spirit infuses each one of our neighbors on earth.

Toward the end of his book *Just Mercy*, Bryan Stevenson recalls how on the steps of a courthouse he met an older black lady wearing a church meeting hat. She said, "My sixteen-year-old grandson was murdered fifteen years ago, and I loved that boy more than life itself." Some boys were found guilty for killing her grandson. She thought their conviction would make her feel better but actually it made her feel worse. A woman came over as the trial concluded and let her lean on her shoulder. The woman asked if the boys convicted were hers, and she said no, the boy they killed was hers. Then she said, "I think she sat with me for almost two hours. For well over an hour, we didn't neither one of us say a word. It felt good to finally have someone to lean on at that trial, and I've never forgotten that woman.... About a year later I started coming down here. I don't really know why. I guess I felt like maybe I could be someone, you know, that somebody hurting could lean on." Then she said these words:

When I first came, I'd look for people who had lost someone to murder or some violent crime. Then it got to the point where some of the ones grieving the most were the ones whose children or parents were on trial, so I just started letting anybody lean on me who needed it. All these young children being sent to prison forever, all this grief and violence. Those judges throwing people away like they're not even human, people shooting each other, hurting each other like they don't care. I don't know, it's a lot of pain. I decided that I was supposed to be here to catch some of the stones people cast at each other."

Then she said to Bryan, "I heard you in that courtroom today. I've even seen you here a couple of times before. I know [you're] a stonecatcher, too" (307–9).

That's what a neighbor does. Catch stones—and sit for two hours as a shoulder to lean on. The first, catch stones, is what Jesus did on the cross. The second, come to us and offer us a shoulder to lean on, is what he does forever. Bryan is a stonecatcher; Lou is a shoulder. Together they demonstrate what it means to be with the neighbor.

CHAPTER 7

Being with Organizations

A group of people gathering together out of common interest is an association. A collection of people, customs, and usually buildings that develop a public identity that transcends time, and is seen by most as constituting a good in itself beyond what it produces, is an institution. Everything that fills the gap between the two is an organization.[1]

Organizations are seen by many of their owners, employees, participants, clients, and customers as being like associations—only good for what you can get out of them; to be used, with no thought or reason to enjoy. But at the same time, as they gain venerability of age, status, and influence, they can come to take on many of the characteristics of institutions as insiders and outsiders look to them to model

---

1. All these terms are contested. Here (and elsewhere in this and the subsequent chapters) I'm offering my own definitions. The books I've found most helpful in exploring these matters are Charles Handy, *Understanding Organizations*, 4th ed. (London: Penguin, 1993); Stephen Pattison, *The Faith of the Managers: When Management Becomes Religion* (London: Continuum, 1997); Hugh Heclo, *On Thinking Institutionally* (Boulder: Paradigm, 2008); and John McKnight and Peter Block, *The Abundant Community: Awakening the Power of Families and Neighborhoods* (San Francisco: Berrett-Koehler Publishers, 2010).

trust, reliability, dignity, and good practice. Before exploring what it means to be with organizations, it's important to get a sense of what the dynamics are that make organizations work. Chief among those is management.

When Moses was trying to distribute manna in the wilderness, he realized energy and charisma weren't enough on their own: he needed organization—and so God called seventy elders to help him (Num. 11:16–30). This is the first level of management, which involves cooperation and planning to get a big job done—ensuring all the resources available reach their desired recipients with the appropriate balance between money, time, and quality. But beyond that comes a second level, which we could call the science of management. This was perhaps first characterized by the late-nineteenth-century Quaker engineer Frederick Taylor. He broke work down into segments, introduced time and motion studies, found ways to rationalize job requirements and job-learning time, and succeeded in greatly increasing production and profits. But Taylorism, as it became known, depersonalized the workforce and regarded workers as replaceable units, thus giving management a mixed reputation. In the last hundred years there has emerged what we might call the art of management. Fashions have swung between a more personal emphasis, which has concentrated on teamwork, motivation, staff appraisal, supervision, and collective goal-setting, and a more systemic approach, which emphasizes customer focus, using values rather than rules, and enjoys slogans such as "Culture eats strategy for breakfast."

Reactions to management tend to vary depending on which understanding of management is in question and where people find themselves in an organization. In simple terms management offers to enhance efficiency, economy, and effectiveness, and it's hard to say that these aren't commendable, provided they don't jeopardize other good things.

There's no doubt that some people are more inclined to system and structure than others, and that any organization, to function well, needs a well-thought-out and well-monitored way of doing things. The word "formal" simply means a culture where the guidelines and expectations are transparent; "informal" may sound relaxed, but it may equally indicate a community where the rules are seldom articulated but are nonetheless assumed. Likewise it goes without saying that skills and techniques of such organization can be studied, learned, shared, and improved. This much is hardly controversial.

There are three related areas where controversy or confusion arises in relation to organizational management. The first is in the use of similar and overlapping terminology. There is, to start with, a difference between leadership and management. In the words of Field Marshal Lord Slim, "Leadership is of the spirit, compounded of personality and vision; its practice is an art. Management is of the mind, a matter of accurate calculation ... its practice is a science. Managers are necessary; leaders are essential."[2] But there is too much mythology around these distinctions. Leaders can seldom function well without good managers around them; leadership is particularly important in rapidly changing circumstances, and less so in stable periods; management involves elements of leadership; and some styles of leadership are, appropriately, hard to distinguish from good management.

A more subtle distinction is that between management and administration. Administration is largely about rules and procedures. The key is to produce and replicate processes that can be followed in every circumstance. The culture is institutional, the background professional rather than commercial. When we find it oppressive and burdensome, slow

2. Pattison, *Faith of the Managers*, 31.

or impersonal, we call it bureaucracy. The key point is that administration is in the interest of order and consistency. It's hard to measure success. By contrast, management is about results, about improvement, about value for money. It tends toward the organization, which is nimble and malleable and has no unshakeable identity, rather than the institution, which is more based on trust, reliability, and sustainability. Organizations, run by managers, are always in danger of losing their soul (some would interject, "if they had one in the first place"). Institutions, run by administrators, are always in danger of failing to adapt to the times and the prevailing culture. Much of the dynamic in the mainline church at the moment is a typical case of professionals worrying that managers are going to jeopardize the soul of their institution, while managers fear that unless organizational features are introduced the institution will simply die. It's a battle between anxiety and complacency in which there's no winner.

A second area of controversy is the tension between the great and the good. When management becomes a science or an art, it can base its appeal on confidence in a compelling technique that promises to achieve a level of perfection. It speaks of excellence and uses ambitious terms like "total quality management." It offers to turn the clumsy and recalcitrant business of getting the best out of staff into a seamless triumph of year-on-year improvement. It sees the past in general—and patient, abiding relationships with clients or customers in particular—as lazy, ignorant, or complacent, and it speaks with utmost expectation of driving up standards and surpassing challenging targets. Many of these targets may indeed be achieved. But the cost can be that people's sense of the value of what they are doing can be diminished, an atmosphere of constant anxiety, perpetual rush, and lingering fear can spread, and what may sometimes have been resignation from the client or customer may be replaced by restless and even insatiable discontent. At its most extreme the aura of management can develop cult-like qualities, with exalted gurus dispensing mythological theories and blind adherence expected from devoted disciples.

The transformation of the British National Health Service from an institution that was far from perfect but of which people were proud into an organization that's perceived as constantly failing to achieve targets is an example of this tension. If the techniques of management don't produce tangible and perceptible improvements in a community, their imposition can be experienced simply as an unwelcome exercise of power and a relentless impulse to change. Becoming great may seem a distant illusion, while remaining good may feel like a neglected memory. When people say, "This isn't the profession I thought I was entering thirty years ago," this is often the kind of thing they mean. It's a sense sometimes reflected among clergy whose sense of purpose resides in a network of trusting relationships and who find they're being held to account for a number of objectives they haven't always agreed to and don't always share.

A third controversial area is about the view management has of human nature. The early management thinkers such as Frederick Taylor tended toward a rather suspicious view of human character as inclined to be lazy, deceitful, and neglectful. In this vein, management is about scrutiny, a reward structure, and a competitive environment that encourages winners and punishes losers or heel-draggers. In eras more inclined to a positive view of the human spirit, such as the 1920s and the 1960s, management becomes about affirmation, information, and setting an upbeat work environment. The difference is a theological one: Augustine of Hippo made the case that our human problem is perversity. We pride ourselves on our ability to choose, but what we don't realize is we've lost the ability to make good choices. We can't help ourselves. Irenaeus argued that the human predicament was ignorance and immaturity. With the right moral formation and inspiring teachers we can choose well and learn to do good.

A good manager realizes you need a bit of both, although it helps to make the carrot a lot more visible than the stick. Old-fashioned education assumed Augustine's view and worked with discipline, order, and assessment to train the troublesome child into the ways of enlightenment and truth. My own elementary school took the opposite approach: it believed in sending us out into small "bays" to be expressive and creative. In fact we played cards and gambled. While needing such scrutiny and supervision, almost every worker resents it; yet when targets are set, almost everyone seeks further guidance on what meeting those expectations might involve and require. Management is a practice of assuming and encouraging the best in people while anticipating and guarding against the worst.

Thus in society in general, the advantages of management are fairly obvious. It is a series of practices designed to help an organization to achieve its goals more successfully. Good management harnesses the "hard" skills of process and evaluation to the "soft" skills of motivation and teambuilding. It can go wrong when it becomes an arcane science or a dark art that loses sight of the true purpose of an organization and people's reasons for being connected with it, or if it takes too exalted or too suspicious a view of human nature. Indeed, the key to good management is to know its place. It's not the same as leadership: it's an excellent way of getting toward a goal, but it's not usually the best way of determining what that goal should be. Management is a good way of implementing and evaluating change, but it may not be the best judge of whether change is required. It's an established way of reaching tangible, measurable targets, but it may be neglectful, inhospitable, or even corrosive toward intangible, inexpressible, but nonetheless deeply held ideals and principles. It can create a busy atmosphere of fixing problems, but it may have few answers when a challenge is not a problem and is something that can't be fixed. It may be impatient with what it sees as the tired habits of administration, but it may have few ways to reassure those who fear that core values and identity may be in jeopardy.

These are among the key areas of tension and enquiry when it comes to understanding organizations. There's no doubt many among congregations, church staff, and clergy feel much more comfortable amid associations and institutions rather than organizations. Associations—gatherings of those who have a common interest—tend to be highly relational environments where task seldom obscures the wider benefits of being involved, such as friendship, fellow-feeling, and fun. (When people say "the church isn't just a club for the like-minded" or a "holy huddle," they're saying it's a lot more than an association.) Meanwhile institutions are cultures with noble ideals, a long-range vision, and patience about translating good intentions into tangible outcomes. Thus many churchgoers relate more easily to associations and institutions than to organizations, which are more characterized by short-term targets, constant evaluation, competitiveness, and highly specific, perhaps narrow, metrics.

So, before moving to the dimensions of being with, it's worth pausing to identify the anxiety many in the church have about organizations and the management practices that permeate them. Should the church regard management as an indispensable asset, a critical friend, or a dangerous threat? The answer depends on an understanding of the church's nature and purpose. If we take one traditional answer, the saving of souls, then management is potentially an indispensable asset. Clergy and lay people preach, witness, invite, persuade, and share—and management helps them do this more cheaply, more effectively, and thus more extensively. But that has never been the church's only purpose. The church also seeks to meet God in gathered worship, pastoral encounter, and mission interface; it seeks to shape its life according to the ways of righteousness and truth; it seeks to grow in character, understanding, and spirit as well as in numbers; it seeks, in the world, justice and peace in relation to the oppressed and the planet; most succinctly, it seeks to glorify and enjoy God forever—and this is only a brief survey. Management can help it achieve many, perhaps most of these goals: it can set priorities, learn from experience, motivate teams, share wisdom, develop strategies, and much more. But management can't determine which of these goals is the most important or prevent them sometimes cutting across one another. And when the assiduous implementation of one goal impedes the less articulate or energized pursuit of another, it's useless to blame "management" as if it were a truck running out of control across a highway. A truck is an implement; it becomes a demon only if it's switched on but has no driver. Management is an instrument, and it can be an instrument of God's peace; it becomes a problem only when it becomes an ultimate good, and end in itself, and if that happens in the church it can only be because of the church's own failure to establish and agree and pursue more appropriate goals.

Thus management is, at its best, a critical friend to the church. The church is full of ideals, some glorious, others impossible; some beautiful, others hypocritical; some insightful, others contradictory; some radical, others ridiculous. The church believes that, in Jesus, it has the words of eternal life; but it also recognizes, with Paul, that love does not insist on its own way. And management does no more and no less than say, or perhaps whisper, or if necessary shout, "Who do you need to help you with this? Which part do you need to do first, and which part can wait? Who else needs to know, and whose insight or energy would it be neglectful to overlook? How can we find a way to make this skill transferable to those to whom it doesn't come easily? How can we make this fun and rewarding and not just pious and dutiful? How can we pay for it without shortage of money derailing our intentions? How can we make sure all this happens even if something significant goes wrong on the way?" These are questions that organizational management asks every day but that the church has often been poor at addressing. To suggest such questions don't matter or are mindless interference is simply to lack humility and humanity. And it risks losing a wonderful friend, because that friend believes in accountability and follow-through, two things the church should believe in.

Jesus describes himself as the vine, and the Father, interestingly, as what the French call a *vigneron*, or vine dresser, and what might best be called the manager. Jesus calls the disciples to their true purpose: he says, "Abide in me." But he also says, "Bear much fruit" (John 15:1–8). To do this second thing requires the work of the vine dresser, who prunes the tree and clears away the branches and puts them on the fire. For Christians the central purpose is to abide in Christ. But to fulfill their further calling—to bear much fruit—they need to get organized, and they need some help, and they need to learn some new skills. And the word for getting organized, and needing some help, and learning new skills, is "management."

I've considered management at length because so much of the church looks upon it with such suspicion, not to say disdain, and because I want to highlight that what many seek as a simpler, less worldly form of ministry is actually a desire to be part of an association or an institution rather than an organization. The church is never simply an organization; but if

it doesn't incorporate some features of organizational thinking, it risks erosion through complacency and inflexibility.

To be with organizations it's important to be mindful of
both role and context. By role I mean that there are broadly
three locations from which one can offer incarnational engagement. One is where an outsider, usually with ministerial accreditation, takes up a recognizable responsibility as
a chaplain. Chaplains are more commonly associated with
institutions, such as hospitals, prisons, military units, or
schools; but the same principles can apply to organizations
too: examples may be a major league football or baseball
team, a retail chain, or a factory. A chaplain is a visible representative of the church, who is in but not of the organization in question. What such a person is actually there to
do, who pays his or her wages, and whether his or her presence is problematic (in an often competitive, fast-paced, and
religiously plural culture) are questions that perpetually
surface. This is an explicitly being-with role, subject to the
misunderstandings and temptations of all such roles: the
misunderstandings are that a person in such a role is irrelevant, in the way, and constantly making negative judgments;
the temptation is for the person to be more active and useful individually by lapsing into patterns of working with or
working for. Thus a chaplain, in an effort to seem effective
and helpful, may establish a role as consultant on interfaith
disputes in the workplace, or an advisor on mental health and
well-being. Such things are valuable in their own right, but
they can become substitutes for or subtle avoidance methods
for genuine being with.

Another location, more suitable for such consultancy,
is that of a critical friend, most commonly sought out by
the senior leaders of the organization themselves but not
in any formal way part of the organizational structure. It's
unlikely that one would be invited into a role like this ex-

plicitly because one is a disciple; but disciples may nonetheless be asked to take on such roles because of their professional suitability. Those who fill the role of a critical friend can adopt many of the practices of being with—attention, mystery, delight, partnership, enjoyment—without concentrating on presence and participation in the way a chaplain would do. They would most likely not be a public representative of the church; they would bring to the conversation a range of perspectives and qualities, of which incarnational Christian faith would be one; and they would usually address specific issues rather than the community as a whole. The temptations here are to retreat into working with and even being for—for example by having little or no contact with the employees or regular participants in the organization themselves—to the detriment of being with; and of the faith component of the consultancy to disappear altogether in the rush to help the organization succeed or survive.

A third location, one that takes participation and presence as key, is to be with by becoming an active participant in the organization itself as an employee, senior executive, shareholder, or board member (and specifically not as chaplain). This has fairly obvious advantages and disadvantages. The advantages are thorough knowledge and understanding of and exposure to the organization. The disadvantages are having a specific role that is not to be with, being in a collaborative but also competitive relationship with colleagues, and very limited opportunity to think or engage outside the organization. In short, the advantage is immersion, the disadvantage is submersion. Nonetheless, almost every role in any organization offers at least some opportunities to practice being with; confusion of role can be a damaging source of manipulation, misunderstanding, and mistrust—but is often simply a fact of life, in which relationships are seldom as straightforward as an organizational chart.

Turning to context, we can envisage five broad scenarios within which one may be seeking to be with an organization. Rather than explore what all eight dimensions of being with mean in each scenario, I shall highlight which themes seem most pertinent to each respective context.

The first is, happily, when all is well, for the organization and the individuals within it. That doesn't mean there are no healthy tensions, challenging deadlines, staff leaving and arriving, or debates about direction, strategy, delegation, investment, growth, economic climate, and innovation. Such are the stuff of organizational life. Endless research and resultant theory has gone into what makes things go well. One of the best-known models is Meredith Belbin's account of what makes a good team. He argues that teams need a balanced chair, a dominant shaper, an innovative plant, an analytical monitor-evaluator, a sociable resource-investigator, a methodical company worker, a harmonizing team worker, and a relentless finisher.[3] The point of such models for our purposes is to anticipate the diversity that success requires and the inevitable tension and adaptation that such diversity involves. Another influential model speaks of two groups of corporate characteristics: the "cold triangle" of strategy, structure, and systems, and the "warm square" of superordinate goals (or shared values), staff, skills, and style, within which shared values governs the flourishing of the other six elements, all of which are indispensable.[4] The point to be derived from this model is that there's no single element (such as strong leadership) that makes an organization flourish— it takes the cultivation of good practices and relationships across a spectrum of interactions. At the same time the no-

3. R. M. Belbin, *Management Teams* (London: Heinemann, 1981).

4. R. Pascale and A. Athos, *The Art of Japanese Management: Applications for American Executives* (New York: Simon & Schuster, 1981).

tion of "group-think" offers a warning to the elevation of shared values. Irving Janis describes how perfectly competent teams could make terrible mistakes because they placed too great a value on the harmony of the group. He observes how groups would overestimate their ability, explain away contrary evidence, stereotype enemies, pressure doubters to keep silent, self-censor doubts, screen out dissent, and prize collective responsibility. Janis gives the example of what John F. Kennedy learned from the Bay of Pigs—which meant that when it came to the Cuban missile crisis he pulled together a more diverse group with greater testing of alternatives and openness to conflicting evidence.[5] Again, Janis's point is that success and harmony are not the same thing.

Being with organizations in fair weather is largely about **delight** and **enjoyment**. I've tried to model that delight in my earlier remarks about management: so much theological observation of organizations is critical, skeptical, even ungenerous and self-righteous. Organizations bring about untold good; of course they can be partly flawed or even wholly malign—but they are the principal way in which people gather their energies, skills, and resources to bring about mutual and societal profit and improvement. This anecdote from the organizational guru Charles Handy makes the point vividly:

> I once facetiously described a rowing eight as a typical British group—eight people going backwards without talking to each other, steered by the one person who was too small to see where they were going. I was sternly rebuked by an oarsman in the audience. "They are the perfect example of a good team," he said. "They would not have the confidence to pull at the oar so strongly without either talking

5. I. L. Janis, *Victims of Groupthink: A Psychological Study of Foreign-Policy Decisions and Fiascoes* (Boston: Houghton Mifflin, 1972).

or seeing if they did not have complete trust in each other and the little person at the rudder." I stood rebuked.[6]

When organizations work well they are analogies of church and kingdom. Consider the origin of the word "company" in the companionship of breaking bread together; reflect on how the word "corporation" indicates a body. The organizing metaphor for Christian collectives is the body of Christ:

> For just as the body is one and has many members, and all the members of the body, though many, are one body, so it is with Christ.... If the foot would say, "Because I am not a hand, I do not belong to the body," that would not make it any less a part of the body. And if the ear would say, "Because I am not an eye, I do not belong to the body," that would not make it any less a part of the body. If the whole body were an eye, where would the hearing be? If the whole body were hearing, where would the sense of smell be? ... But God has so arranged the body, giving the greater honor to the inferior member, that there may be no dissension within the body, but the members may have the same care for one another. If one member suffers, all suffer together with it; if one member is honored, all rejoice together with it. Now you are the body of Christ and individually members of it. (1 Cor. 12:12–27)

Delight means appreciating how applicable this passage is to the workings of any organization, and how experience of and appreciation for the workings of, say, a production line, or a supply chain, can illustrate and deepen understanding

6. Handy, *Understanding Organizations*, 152.

of this passage. Paul affirms that it takes many and diverse members to make a body. He recognizes how hierarchies and pecking orders work and how the ear should not feel inferior to the eye: each part has a vital role to play. Just as no one has any need to say, "I do not belong," likewise no one gets to say, "I have no need of you"—not the eye to the hand or the head to the feet. The research and models of Belbin, Pascale, Janis, and others are all anticipated here in Paul's epistles. There are different roles—apostles, prophets, teachers, deeds of power, gifts of healing, assistance, leadership, and tongues—and all of them are indispensable. No one has the time, the capability, or the authority to carry out all of these roles on one's own. No group can ever say it's made it. All organizations are provisional. Diversity is a gift and a strength, not a weakness or a sign of unfaithfulness. Unity is something an organization has to work at, and that work is not a distraction but is the key to its flourishing. The qualitative difference about the church, for Paul, is that the Spirit gave baptism and the drink of empowerment, and that God arranged and appointed roles. This doesn't mean the church isn't an organization—it shares significant common features of the kind we've explored—but it clearly means it's an organization of a different kind.

Delight works on a micro and a macro level. On a micro level it's as simple as expressing appreciation. B. F. Skinner recognized that positive reinforcement should be specific, immediate, based on achievable targets, and unpredictable (rather than anticipated) because most people value attention and recognition more than financial rewards.[7] Such analysis takes the joy and spontaneity out of delight, but highlights how important delight nonetheless is. On a

7. B. F. Skinner, *Beyond Freedom and Dignity* (Cambridge, MA: Hackett, 1971), quoted in Handy, *Understanding Organizations*, 228.

macro level delight means discerning and celebrating the sustainable and surprising goods of an organization and the value of each member. In one organization in London there were around twenty-five different nationalities represented on a staff team of around 135. When the result of the Brexit referendum was announced in June 2016, many of those staff members heard the vote for the UK to leave the European Union as a statement of personal rejection that problematized and jeopardized their belonging in England. The leadership of the organization arranged a multicultural evening that celebrated the different cultural identities and illustrated tangible and intangible ways the organization was richer, deeper, and healthier for its diverse workforce. This was an exercise in delight.

Enjoyment is perhaps the most intriguing dimension of being with an organization because an organization may be described as something that is explicitly set up to use rather than to enjoy. An organization is by definition a means to an end. It's almost never an end in itself: it's the most effective way to make money, achieve political change, raise awareness of an issue, reduce waste on the streets, protect vulnerable people, provide childcare—or any of a myriad assortment of purposes. This is perhaps the most vivid distinction between an organization and an institution: an institution is created to be enjoyed, as an end in itself, to appreciate art, shape the practice of law, teach ballet, heal the sick; by contrast, an organization is created to be used as a means to an end, a ladder than can be kicked away once the end is reached. But in practice almost every institution has organizational features, and many organizations acquire, over time, institutional qualities. Some notions of organization notably lack the dimension of enjoyment altogether; notoriously, Taylorism argued that there was an almost universal law that those equipped to serve a trade cannot understand the science of that trade without the "kindly help and cooperation" of more educated people. This sees a whole class of people as fit only to be used. But this tendency isn't universal. In general it's a mistake to draw too sharp a distinction between organizations and institutions.

To enjoy an organization is to perceive not just what it is but what it can be, not just what it has to be to get the job done but what it touches on in its transcendent moments of cooperation, innovation, initiative, improvisation, commitment, dedication, selflessness, and inspiration. It is to be resolved never to take anything for granted, but to relish every detail of what it takes to achieve a goal. Leadership gurus love to tell the story of John F. Kennedy's visit to Cape Canaveral when, it's said, he met two housekeepers. He said to each of them, "What do you do?" One answered, "I keep this place nice and tidy"; while the other said, solemnly, "I'm putting a man on the moon." (The story is said to be based on a seventeenth-century fable about the building of St. Paul's Cathedral in London, when Christopher Wren approached two stonemasons, one of whom said, "I'm carving stone," while the other said, "I'm building the house of God.") The point is not the feel-good familiarity of the story, but the recognition that in each case the first person thought only to use, whereas the second person knew what it meant to enjoy.

Since it is not always fair weather in organizations, it's time to explore what it means to be with organizations in other seasons. One is the context of corporate struggle or failure when there is no wrongdoing, simply a change in economic climate, the market, competitors, and demand—external and unavoidable circumstances. All organizations finish or fail for one reason or another, and, to the extent that people invest identity and well-being in them as if they were associations or institutions—let alone financial investment and employment—their demise evokes grief and distress. Being with in such a situation means **participation**; it involves solidarity. If the company is going to the wall and the official receivers are in a position to introduce a potential buyer, and a bunch of local people are planning to picket the receivers to make their feelings known about what the survival of the company means to the town, being with means accompanying the local people—not particularly to affect the outcome of negotiations but simply to say, "I have observed the misery of my people . . . ; I have heard their cry on account of their taskmasters. Indeed, I know their sufferings" (Exod. 3:7). It's not an apportionment of blame; it's an acknowledgment of pain. It's not a time for recrimination, the claiming of special insight or neglected expertise; it's a statement that organizations are made up of human beings, and too often when they fail they collapse on top of their employees. Being with means recalling the words of John Donne:

> No man is an island, entire of itself; every man is a piece of the continent, a part of the main. If a clod be washed away by the sea, Europe is the less, as well as if a promontory were, as well as if a manor of thy friend's or of thine own were: any man's death diminishes me, because I am involved in mankind, and therefore never send to know for whom the bell tolls; it tolls for thee.[8]

Participation is a tangible manifestation and articulation that "It tolls for me too."

Often, however, the circumstances are different, and there's a humiliation, shame, or reduction of circumstances, arising from one person losing a job or being excluded in

8. John Donne, "Meditation 17," in *Devotions upon Emergent Occasions and Death's Duel* (New York: Vintage Books, a Division of Random House, 1999), 103.

some other way from an organization and consequently facing an unknown, unstable, and perhaps impoverished future. In addition to financial insecurity, redundancy can diminish the color and activity of life, dismantle the structure of the day, disempower decision-making, allow skills to atrophy, undermine confidence, reduce the range of informal acquaintances, and shrink self-worth. Being with a person who's been laid off involves, fundamentally, **presence** alongside a person who may very likely feel abandoned. It says, "Everyone else may have left you, changed their opinion of you, been too embarrassed to speak to you, hidden their face from you, avoided you, scoffed at you, felt guilty that it was you and not them, tried to avoid thinking depressing thoughts that you triggered in them, denied responsibility for you: but I'm still here. And I'll go on being here, because my estimation of you is not based on your salary, résumé, job title, influence, experience, or even wisdom, but on who you are in the sight of God, who made you, redeemed you, and abides with you, whether or not you recognize it or find that knowledge helpful." Every gesture of presence is a sacramental instantiation of God's presence with us in Christ and the Holy Spirit; all the more so when there's nothing to say. Gifts or advice may be unwise—they may appear to be avoidance of the reality that there's nothing you can do to make things better: the challenge is to have the courage to show up empty-handed and empty-mouthed. The best way to show others that they are valuable in and of themselves is to come to see them bringing nothing but oneself. In the end there is nothing but companionship and relationship—all else is ancillary to being with: here is a profound moment of turning convictions about eternity into practical actions today.

Presence is inestimably valuable for its own sake. But within abiding, repeated, regular presence is an attitude of **mystery**. There is, first of all, the mystery of a human being:

fearfully and wonderfully made, glorious in potential, power, beauty, subtlety, skill, passion, adventure, wonder, detail, and dynamism. All these things say that redundancy (or whatever the damaging setback is) does not characterize this person: this person is about so much more, in the past, in the future—and now. There is, alongside the setback, the mystery of disappointment, distress, disadvantage, devastation; all little forms of death—itself a mystery, plausible in biological terms only, otherwise seeming to contradict all that makes for life, and flourishing, and growth, and hope. Accordingly there comes a mystery that's a kind of denial: could there not have been another way, could it not have been gentler, kinder, fairer, more consultative, more gradual, more transparent, more just? But slowly, graciously, ruined by being rushed, there may begin to appear a narrative kind of mystery, God's purpose being worked out, setbacks turning into opportunities, a providential hand—scarred by the nails of the cross, certainly—crafting a new future out of a painful past. The Scriptures are full of such turnarounds, from Joseph's rejection by his brothers to Moses's flight from Pharaoh, from Daniel's punishment by Darius to Mordecai's persecution by Haman, from the holy family's escape to Egypt to Paul's countless hostile receptions. In so many cases what seemed a disaster became the beginning of something previously unimaginable. "I am confident of this, that the one who began a good work among you will bring it to completion by the day of Jesus Christ" (Phil. 1:6). "Therefore the Lord waits to be gracious to you; therefore he will rise up to show mercy to you. For the Lord is a God of justice; blessed are all those who wait for him" (Isa. 30:18).

In the words of John Henry Newman,

> God has created me to do him some definite service; he has committed some work to me which he has not committed

to another. I have my mission—I never may know it in this life, but I shall be told it in the next.

Somehow I am necessary for his purposes. I have a part in this great work; I am a link in a chain, a bond of connection between persons. He has not created me for naught. I shall do good, I shall do his work; I shall be an angel of peace, a preacher of truth in my own place, while not intending it, if I do but keep his commandments and serve him in my calling.

Therefore I will trust him. Whatever, wherever I am, I can never be thrown away. If I am in sickness, my sickness may serve him; in perplexity, my perplexity may serve him; if I am in sorrow, my sorrow may serve him. My sickness, or perplexity, or sorrow may be necessary causes of some great end, which is quite beyond us. He does nothing in vain; he may prolong my life, he may shorten it; he knows what he is about. He may take away my friends, he may throw me among strangers, he may make me feel desolate, make my spirits sink, hide the future from me—still he knows what he is about.[9]

There is very little access to mystery without patience. And mystery is sometimes another word for hope. But it is perhaps the only way to **glory**.

There are still two further scenarios to explore. One is when the corporation as a whole fails morally, either by not establishing high standards or by not living up to them. This can be for various reasons. It can stem from ignorance, for example when a company board disregards its potential for leadership on ecological issues, or when it fails to discern a

9. John Henry Newman, "Meditations on Christian Doctrine," meditation 1, "Hope in God—Creator," March 7, 1848, in *Meditations and Devotions of the Late Cardinal Newman* (New York: Longmans, Green, and Co., 1903), 301–2.

sinister culture of undermining remarks and gestures that make life for women in the workplace distressing and inhospitable. It can arise from neglect, as when lack of close supervision or structures of accountability make it possible for bullying or fraud to be perpetrated frequently within the organization. It can come out of a narrow, entirely instrumental view of the workforce, when the balance of coercion and cooperation is skewed toward the former and sharp practices are habitually used to make the work environment abrasive or even dangerous, or when executive pay is allowed to reach levels absurdly greater than the remuneration level of the great majority of the staff. But it can also be rooted in conscious, willed, collective misconduct, for instance when a product is doctored so it doesn't contain the ingredients it claims to, or if tax evasion (rather than avoidance) becomes a corporate policy.

In these circumstances being with an organization as chaplain, critical friend, or participant is about **partnership**. It's seldom about being a self-styled prophet, awaiting the moment to denounce, embarrass, shame, and expose. Such a view of mission adopts a view of speaking truth to power that assumes one has all the truth oneself and the organization has all the power; it risks the grail of relationship, cherishing, and the possibility of transformation for the gratification of public attention, shock, and instant reaction. It's therefore a last resort that jettisons being with in favor of being for. Partnership, as ever, is largely a working-with relationship where each party has something important and irreplaceable to contribute. There are many good reasons to seek honorable practice on the part of the organization: ones based in duty, like honesty, fair play, and dignity, but also ones shaped by sober calculation, such as public perception, sustainability of a brand, loyalty and commitment of a workforce, and attractiveness to likely recruits. Being with can involve saying, "It may be that I can help you align your short-term temptations with your long-term goals." It could mean wondering, "Have you recently done a staff survey to check what your employees are really thinking and what changes they would really value?" It can include asking, "What do think your customers most value about your brand, and how damaging might it be if they found out a little bit more about how things work here?" Sometimes asking questions is all that partnership requires, so long as one has the patience to wait around for answers and the persistence to keep asking. The point is to see the kingdom as always coming—never (by one's own hand) complete, or fully arrived; being with an organization in partnership is about seeking to help it grow, develop, and if necessary change in order more nearly to resemble the kingdom—not about demanding that it turn into the kingdom tomorrow. And if the change is going to be deep and lasting, it needs to come from within; working for—campaigning for imposed change from outside—is seldom the answer.

Finally there is the scenario where the wrongdoing has been not corporate but individual. "The Lord said to Cain, 'Why are you angry, and why has your countenance fallen? If you do well, will you not be accepted? And if you do not do well, sin is lurking at the door; its desire is for you, but you must master it'" (Gen. 4:6–7). Ideally an organization creates a culture and accountability structure by which an individual who seeks only to use either the organization, a fellow employee, or a client, and not to honor or enjoy them, will be intercepted before great harm is done; made aware of standards, commitments, and consequences; convinced of a better way; and rehabilitated without damage to any third party or themselves. But it is not always so. And widespread hurt, loss, injustice, and harm can result. The heart of being with in this context is **attention**. Attention means detailed work to ensure others, who might not be so inclined, carefully and thoroughly establish, codify, and communicate the way people are to inhabit the organization, lest there be any misunderstanding; it means putting practices and structures of accountability in place with clear rewards and penalties, a bias toward rehabilitation but a recognition that forgiveness need not always mean waiving an appropriate punishment; and it means conscientious follow-through, to ensure worthy policies are actually carried out and promises not to do it again are kept and reparative actions are truly made.

These are all acts of anticipation. Preparation, it is often said, is two-thirds of any venture. But when the systems have failed and people have let themselves and the organization down, whether by ignorance, weakness, or their own deliberate fault, being with requires careful attention. Not ostracism; not berating; not repeated demands to know "Why?" Tempting as all these might be, they are all forms of lack of attention, reluctance to dwell in the pain and the mess and the mystery of transgression. What's fundamentally wrong with sin, enjoying what should be used and using what should be enjoyed, is that it makes being with difficult or impossible. Thus the way to overcome sin is through being with, in all its dimensions; and in circumstances of wrongdoing in an organization, that means detailed attention, exhaustive (if necessary) naming of instances of transgression, and close recognition of all that was not corrupted and offers fertile soil from which may grow redemption. Being with doesn't replace calling to account, censure, apology, correction, punishment, and a visible changing of ways: but it does seek to ensure that such measures are undertaken genuinely rather than perfunctorily, that neither the organization not the transgressor loses sight of the restorative and relational dimensions of the process, and that a culture of "paying one's dues" is replaced by one that aims for growth, transformation, and reconciliation.

Theologians and popes have often called the family a mini-church—though evidently it is frequently not experienced as such. One could describe an organization as a mini-kingdom—with the same corollary. In many ways, being so task-driven, so given to use rather than to enjoy, organizations may seem abrasive to being with; all the more reason for being with to rise to the challenge, in the foregoing ways and many more.

CHAPTER 8

Being with Institutions

An institution embodies or comes to signify a collection of commitments, practices, and aspirations that people cherish because they elevate them above their own regular wants and needs to something of deeper and more lasting value and abiding worth. For disciples, the most significant thing about institutions is that they share many things in common with church. Thus being with institutions has both the impulse to uphold qualities of genuine importance and enduring validity and a slight anxiety that in doing so one is affirming the human endeavor to ground honor in something other than God.

On the one hand are the words, "Beloved, let us love one another, because love is from God; everyone who loves is born of God and knows God. Whoever does not love does not know God, for God is love" (1 John 4:7-8). These sentiments are amplified by the ninth-century Latin hymn, "Ubi caritas et amor, Deus ibi est" (Where charity and love are found, there is God). Together they encourage the view that institutions, at their best, are concrete, sustainable forms of love. On the other hand are Jesus's words, "Whoever is not with me is against me, and whoever does not gather with me scatters" (Matt. 12:30), taken by Cyprian of Carthage to mean "Outside the Church there is no salvation"; which is simply to say, an institution may exhibit many good features—but it is not the church. An institution is invested in things of enduring value; but it does not necessarily recognize that here we have no abiding city, since we seek the city that is to come. An institution requires and fosters the development of virtues; but alongside courage, prudence, justice, and temperance, it doesn't always thereby foster faith, hope, and love. An institution may celebrate the wonder of human achievement; but it may thereby exalt the grass that withers and the flower that fades rather than the word of God that lasts forever.

An institution arises when a group of people recognize both the value of certain traditions, activities, or social goods and the fallible, fragile, and transitory character of individual lives—and so seek to invest in a collective body to uphold precious things that rise above the day-to-day vulnerability of human weakness. Such is an art museum, a university, an orchestra. Institutions are similar in many respects to organizations (and there are many hybrids, with features of both, such as hospitals); the difference is that institutions cultivate substantive goods, such as beauty, trust, and wisdom, whereas organizations are largely restricted to instrumental goods such as income-generation and the attainment of other tangible goals and targets. An organization, being shaped toward achieving limited, identifiable, practical outcomes, has a flexible, almost chameleon-like quality: it will take whatever form is required to get the job done; it may be gone next year if the job no longer needs doing or another organization purchases, outmaneuvers, or absorbs it. When people lament that a well-known store is no longer to be seen in the mall, they are asking an organization to be something it can't be—a source of social stability, reliability, and permanence that stands strong when "change and decay in all around I see." Interest groups shift around, environmental influences alter the surrounding climate enormously, and organizations transform themselves rapidly either to survive or morph into something else.

By contrast, institutions transcend desire, preference, or convenience and strive for aspirational goals, translating those abstract goals, through detailed attention, into ways of relating that affirm and embody them, exchanging the appropriate for the expedient. The political scientist Hugh Heclo frames the issue in terms of what questions one asks.

> From inside an institutional worldview, one is moved by a central fact—that there is something estimable and decisive beyond me and my immediate personal inclinations. In approaching a major choice, the question is not, How can I get what I want? It is the duty-laden question that asks, What expectations and conduct are appropriate to my position and the choices I might make? What is it, larger than myself, to which I am drawn? And attracted by the light of its value, what should I want? … All institutions offer answers to such questions, questions that modern societies have often forgotten how to ask.[1]

That sense of time is an integral dimension of what institutions mean in society. They are, fundamentally, the way wisdom is handed on from past to future. A neighborhood or whole society that is shorn of institutions has no way of preserving social capital, no way of preventing insight and good practice from dying out with each lone exponent. Institutions are not naïve, idealistic projects ignorant of flawed existence; they are precisely built around human shortcomings

---

1. Hugh Heclo, On Thinking Institutionally (Boulder, CO: Paradigm, 2008), 102–3.

and designed to transcend them. Institutional thinking "insists that mundane life is far more than a banal submission to expediency. It views the present as thoroughly enriched by inheritance and legacy.... [It] tends to humble without humiliating us, to raise us up without flattering us."[2]

Three terms may be taken to characterize institutional life. The first is "profession." The professional-client relationship once relied on a competence-gap in knowledge and practice, and the deference that resulted. It had strong elements of dominance and dependence (what I would term the weaknesses of working for), but there were shared values and goals, such as education and learning. But since the era loosely known as "the sixties," figures like doctors and teachers have increasingly come to be seen as providers of services, and their patients and pupils as consumers of those services. Ratings tables establish hierarchies; litigation awaits those perceived to have failed. What's taking place is that the previously unquestioned status of the institution is becoming incoherent, and expectations abound that it will behave like any other organization.

A second term is "office." Originally, in Cicero's De Officiis, an office was a position in society together with the set of expectations and raft of duties that accompanied it. In medieval times it came to describe those things a priest was expected to do, such as pray the psalms and readings of the hour (the "daily office"). It differs from function or role because the latter make no demands upon the state of the occupant's mind or heart—whereas an office requires the office-holder to give heart and mind and soul and strength to the matter in hand; the doing of it serves a more than practical purpose—it's the doing, rather than getting-done, that's fundamental. I recall asking a surgeon how her work had changed over her twenty

2. Heclo, *On Thinking Institutionally*, 128.

years since qualification. She said, "In the early years, the nurses would say, 'It's 4:40 p.m.—just time to clear up quickly and we can squeeze in one more operation.' Now they say, 'It's 4:40 p.m.—I guess by the time we've tidied up that'll be it for the day.'" What she was describing was how the role of nurse, which had once been an office, had become a job.

The third word is the verb "entrust."[3] An institution is something that no one owns—it is entrusted to those who seek to pass it on to their successors stronger, richer, finer, worthier than they inherited it. It's a profound working-for office. There's no detailed supervision, direct accountability, or clinical analysis. Instead there's trust, patience, expectation, hope. This is something deeper than a relationship of contract; it's a bond of covenant.[4] It's not simply about agreed goals, measurable targets, recognized penalties for inadequate compliance; it's about ultimate purpose, deep conviction, wholehearted commitment. It's not that there's no place for accountability—time, after all, will be the judge—but bureaucratic accountability is as likely to diminish this culture of trust as to strengthen it. Heclo describes this vividly. He says modern society has created a layered system of guardians monitoring guardians, in which procedural compliance replaces genuine calling to account. Yet

adding up micro-accountabilities does not produce macro-accountability. It is in fact more likely than not to obscure it. It is like judging a pitcher's performance by summing

3. Heclo, *On Thinking Institutionally*, 130–49. Heclo speaks of profession, office, and stewardship in terms related to the way I describe them above; I prefer "entrust" to "stewardship" (despite moving from a noun to a verb) because I see "steward" as a thin term for which a theologically richer term would be "priest." See Samuel Wells, *God's Companions: Reimagining Christian Ethics* (Oxford: Blackwell, 2006), 192–95.

4. For more on this distinction, see Samuel Wells, *Learning to Dream Again: Rediscovering the Heart of God* (Grand Rapids: Eerdmans, 2013), 50–55.

up assessments of each one of his pitches. That never tells you the important big thing, which is whether he won the game.... Our society is clogged with multiple accountability processes to the point of dissolving ... responsibility into nonexistence. This is done in a vain effort to control the discretionary actions of people whom we put into positions of trust, and then do everything possible to show that we do not consider them trustworthy.[5]

Heclo points out the countercultural nature of institutions in a postmodern intellectual climate by contrasting the Harvard faculty's description of the aims of education with those of renaissance humanism. The Harvard proposal values unsettling presumptions, revealing what is going on behind appearances, disorienting young people and helping them find resources to reorient themselves. Its methods are to question assumptions, to induce self-reflection, to teach analytical and critical thinking, to take them outside their historical and cultural location, and to stretch their capacity to understand. By contrast, the fifteenth-century Italian Pier Paolo Vergerio the Elder regarded as liberal those studies that were worthy of a free man—by which virtue or wisdom could be practiced or sought, and by which body or mind could be shaped to the best things, and by which honor and glory, the rewards of virtue, could be sought. While the illiberal might seek profit and pleasure, the liberal seek glory and virtue.[6] For Heclo, whereas critical thinking dismantles trust and manufactures skepticism, institutional thinking builds up and gives intelligence abiding shape. He quotes with approval the words of Alfred North Whitehead: "It is a profoundly erroneous truism, repeated by all copybooks and by eminent people

5. Heclo, *On Thinking Institutionally*, 148–49.
6. Heclo, *On Thinking Institutionally*, 94–95.

when they are making speeches, that we should cultivate the habit of thinking of what we are doing. The precise opposite is the case. Civilization advances by extending the number of important operations which we can perform without thinking about them."[7]

But there's more that's unfashionable about institutions than an intellectual climate preoccupied with suspicion. The two principal threats to institutions are a culture that prizes individual expression and fulfillment and a climate of skepticism with regard to the integrity of public servants. Hugh Heclo describes two stalemates: one, "between our cultural norm of individual autonomy free from the demands of external authority, and the inescapable need to entrust ourselves to some such authority"; the other, "between the distrust that various institutions have richly earned and the vague appreciation of institutional values that makes possible our sense of betrayal when that has happened."[8] On the one hand there is a widely assumed rule that we should live and let live—in other words, live as we please provided we don't inhibit others doing the same. This philosophy was not always there; writing in 1981, one experienced opinion pollster observed a change from a time when "Americans believed that self-denial made sense, sacrificing made sense, obeying the rules made sense, subordinating the self to the institution made sense." But since the interlude widely known as "the sixties," there has been a different atmosphere. Now many Americans believe that "the old giving/getting compact needlessly restricts the individual while advancing the power of large institutions" and that power is used to take advantage of the public.[9] While this phenomenon largely refers to what I am

7. Heclo, *On Thinking Institutionally*, 97.
8. Heclo, *On Thinking Institutionally*, 43.
9. Daniel Yankelovich, quoted in Heclo, *On Thinking Institutionally*, 35.

calling organizations and government, the fallout reaches institutions also.

Lest one imagine that institutions are the repository of all things right and just and true, it's worth naming ways in which they can be problematic. They can be elitist: a museum of modern art may aspire to the highest standards of culture and public access, but it may also be a showground for the display of wealth, a concourse for pretension, and a public endorsement of privilege. They can be complacent: office holders can forget that their power is given to uphold self-less values and can turn their institution into an association to protect and convene people like themselves, or they can resist all organizational features that might disperse or pop-ularize its concerns for a new generation. In particular some institutions have become notorious for being slow to change in the face of sharper awareness and scrutiny of class, race, and gender exclusion; the phrase "last bastion" is invariably applied in some such way to institutions that have forgot-ten the need to set an example. For example a golf club may behave as an association by wanting to uphold a male-only membership rule; but it may be forgetting that, as host to elite international tournaments, it is a globally accountable institution, and as a business needing to make such events work financially, it needs to develop characteristics of an organization, and in both these senses a male-only rule is unjustifiable and unsustainable. When a university seeks to understand the role of elite sports in its life, it is balancing its national or international role as an institution upholding excellence in education and research, its associational quality of loyalty to the team and enjoyment of success, and its or-ganizational need to recruit students and balance the books. Inevitably sometimes the organizational and associational impulses encroach on or even damage the institutional imperative.

In regard to being with institutions, the role of chaplain is well established and widely recognized (if not universally understood). Universities, schools, prisons, hospitals, the military, and to a lesser extent uniformed agencies such as police and firefighters have long had the presence and engagement of a representative of a faith tradition to enhance spiritual welfare, offer pastoral care, and lead worship as appropriate. While many of these environments have organizational features and are by no means free of the pressure, competitiveness, anxiety, and urgency of an organizational context, institutions in general lend themselves more easily to chaplaincy, because they are typically more used to discussing ultimate purpose (either in theory or, in the case of the emergency services, in regular encounter with life-and-death scenarios), because they are often more focused on process than outcome, and because in many cases they can trace their origins to religious commitments. In short, chaplaincy is more frequently the model of being with for institutions than for organizations because institutions have more features that resemble church, and thus being with feels more like ministry and less like mission. **Presence** is relatively unproblematic: the role is valued, and much can be achieved and demonstrated simply by being visible and engaged with all involved.

Since I had the privilege of being in the role of chaplain to a prestigious American institution for seven years, it seems appropriate at this juncture, at the risk of self-indulgence, to outline what I thought being with meant there.[10] Like many

10. What follows is adapted and abbreviated from Samuel Wells, "Places of Encounter: Hanging Out Where God Shows Up," in *Academic Vocation in the Church and Academy Today: "And with All of Your Mind,"* ed. Shaun C. Henson and Michael J. Lakey (Farnham: Ashgate, 2016), 203–16. For further thoughts on the larger narrative background, see Samuel Wells, *Speaking the Truth: Preaching in a Pluralistic Culture* (Nashville: Abingdon, 2008).

such roles it was a mixture of ministry and mission; the juxtaposition of these two roles tends not to be as jarring in an institution as it can be in an organization or neighborhood. A couple of months after I began work at Duke University as Dean of the Chapel in 2005, I made my most important purchase. It was the chair I would for the next seven years keep in the far corner of my office. That's the chair toward which I would direct all who came for counsel, direction, supervision, study, or conversation. That chair became the focus of my pastoral efforts at Duke. What I started to imagine was the whole institution, all 36,000 people in the community, occupying that chair in the corner of my office.

My father was a pastor. Where I had a chair, he had a sofa. When I was six years old (I can work out the date because it was during the war between India and Pakistan that led to the formation of an independent Bangladesh out of what had previously been East Pakistan), my sister and I dressed up as Bangladeshi refugees. With a great number of blankets and some headgear recycled from the previous year's nativity play, we assembled ourselves outside the front door and timidly rang the doorbell. When my father answered, we muttered, dolefully, "Our husbands are in Dhaka"—referring to the capital of Bangladesh. My father had compassion on us, showed us gently into his study, sat us down on the well-worn sofa, placed himself opposite us in a chair, and asked us helpful questions, like whether we were cold, or frightened, and how long we expected the war to go on, and would we like to stay with him and his family for a few days. In short, he took us a little more seriously and a little more playfully than we took ourselves. Which is exactly what I tried to do for the years I was called to be with Duke University.

Perhaps the majority of the work the pastor does in a pastoral encounter is done before the chair in the corner of the room is occupied. In that spirit I needed to be aware of several things. One was what a chaplain is for. Those people who gather for corporate worship on a Sunday don't do so for themselves alone; they represent the whole population of the neighborhood in which the church building sits. Just as a spire points an entire building to heaven, so a gathered congregation directs the hearts of all the residents of the neighborhood to God. That congregation worships on behalf of everyone in the neighborhood—Christian, other faith, or no explicit faith. The role of the pastor is to blend the diverse energies and idiosyncrasies and commitments and charisms of the gathered community and to make something beautiful out of them—to make the congregation more than the sum of its parts. Meanwhile the pastor also walks the permeable boundary between the gathered community and the wider neighborhood and speaks a language that can help each understand, be challenged, and be enriched by the other. The pastor is there for the whole neighborhood—not just those who identify with the Christian faith. And so being with carries an assumption in every dialogue—whether the conversation be serious or apparently trivial—of helping the person discern his or her role in that interaction between neighborhood and community, that chemistry between Holy Spirit and human heart, that dynamism between divinity made humanity in Christ and humanity not yet made divinity on the last day, that moment of poise and place of encounter called the kingdom of God. And so, as one called to be with the institution, I was there in mission for the whole university, not just in ministry those who looked to the chapel as a focus of faith; not just for the students and faculty but also for the office staff and housekeepers. I couldn't know everyone—but I could try to ensure that everyone knew me. In short, it was a role of incarnational mission that could not be subsumed into incarnational ministry. Such conflicts as I had with alumni and alumnae, in particular those from the divinity school, were in most cases due to the fact that they assumed my job was ministry, whereas I assumed my role was largely, though not wholly, mission.

I needed, as every pastor does, a second element of self-awareness. What I'd learned about myself through my own times of discernment, through my own journeys and through the interactions in which I'd tried to guide others, was my own inner poverty. And I'd learned that the gospel is about those who have discovered that poverty—that need of God. There are those who have poverty thrust upon them—through exploitation, oppression, cruelty, or bad luck. These need redemption. And there are those who have become poor largely at their own hand—through recklessness or foolishness or hastiness or poor judgment. These need forgiveness. Jesus knew the difference between the two, but he surrounded himself with both. And he still does. I came to articulate a motto—"If it can't be happy, make it beautiful." I assumed in every pastoral encounter that this was what I was helping a person see his or her way to doing. And the same was true of the institution as a whole. It wasn't blithely called to make the world "a better place" or render the individual happy. It was called to inhabit a truer, deeper, richer existence.

In addition to self-awareness was the cultural web of projections that cluster around the pastor and lead the first-time visitor to exclaim, "I never expected you, or your office, or your sense of humor, or your perspective on alcohol [or whatever it may be] to be anything like this!" Particularly after coming from England to Duke, I had to learn that my demeanor led many people to assume that I was effortlessly intelligent, unconsciously patronizing, irredeemably stuffy, relentlessly censorious, and unswervingly solemn, as well as addicted to damp weather, royalty, and afternoon tea. In every pastoral encounter I tried to remind myself that I was doubtless bringing an equally absurd and generalized assortment of projections to bear on my perception of my visitor, and so to refrain from hasty judgment as much as possible.

There were also the dynamics of power and status and expectation that were going on when my role and story came into interaction with my visitors' needs and energies. These dynamics can't and perhaps shouldn't be dismantled, so I had to find ways to make them useful to a greater purpose. My visitors' anticipation, or nervousness, or projection was usually hugely helpful. It meant we didn't spend a lot of time with introductory details, and when I asked them to tell me the whole story, they generally did, succinctly and without long digressions. And when I asked them to tell me the story again, this time just including the parts they really wanted to talk about, we could go straight to the point pretty quickly. And when I asked them what's the worst thing that can happen, they usually knew; and when I asked them what's the best thing that can happen, already, within a half-hour sometimes, they were beginning to chart their own way forward. Unlike a lot of pastors, who try to reduce the distance between them and their people by dressing down and having a friendly ambience in their office, I presented myself formally and kept my office looking as tidy as I could because I wanted all my unspoken messages of dress and posture and setting to say, "I'm going to bring all my experience and understanding and prayerful attention to this encounter, and if you tell me the truth, and open your life to the Holy Spirit, then something exciting and wonderful really could happen here."

So what did it mean for a whole institution, in my case Duke University, to be sitting in that chair in the corner of my office? Similar levels of awareness apply to being with an institution.

One is what the institution thinks it is. Fifty years ago Duke was a provincial university. During my first couple of years I talked with as many people as I could about how in the subsequent thirty years Duke was transformed from a provincial college into a truly national university. The answers came down to two. On the one hand the civil rights movement made the South a less foreign place to the rest of the country. It was not just that African Americans could enrich the institution with their wisdom, talent, and grace. It was that a university like Duke ceased to be a place where privileged elites sought to maintain their stranglehold on power, prestige, and routes to political influence, but instead became a theater where a whole new society could be imagined, a laboratory where previously unthought ideas could be tested, a crucible where diverse people, faiths, convictions, and identities could be forged into exciting new configurations. On the other hand there was the most important invention in the history of the American South: air conditioning. Civil rights made it possible for the rest of America to *identify* with a place like Duke. Air conditioning made it possible for the rest of America actually to *live* there. The combination of the two helped to make Duke a truly national university. And during my tenure Duke was becoming a truly global university.

When I became Dean of Duke Chapel I asked, "What is this university for?" In other words, in what way is Duke an institution, and how does it avoid becoming a sprawling organization whose primary orientation is to harness resources and produce goods and services that are highly valued, thus increasing its corporate prestige, but meanwhile gradually lose the quality of its mission in the quantity of its operations? A gentler way of asking the question is to say, "Where is the heart of this university?" There were many candidates to be the answer to that question, because Duke is famous for many things. But I quickly settled on one answer above all others: the undergraduate classroom. Take any other feature of Duke away—its hospital, its athletic teams, its research program, its architecture, even its chapel—and you still have a lot of operating parts; but take away the undergraduates and the faculty, whose raison d'être is most succinctly expressed in the professor-student relationship in the classroom, and you've removed the keystone in the Gothic arch.

From this insight I derived a number of conclusions that guided my ministry at Duke. One was that Duke Chapel should not think of itself as the heart of the university. Others could call us that if they chose, but it should never describe itself in such terms. To do so would suggest it was pining for or even seeking to restore a lost era when Protestant faith went hand in hand with social, economic, political, and cultural dominance, an era when Christian faith became dragooned into and entangled within a social vision that included some and excluded others. That was an era where people confused an institution with a large-scale association. There is a place for Christianity on a campus like Duke, but not if it assumes it is the normal, unquestioned, civil religion everyone should subscribe to. That is to confuse mission and ministry.

So I coined the mission statement, "Keeping the heart of the university listening to the heart of God." This started with a note of continuity ("Keeping") that honored many decades of ministry at the Chapel. It spoke of the "heart of the university" but left open the question of where that heart lay. It used the term "listening" to ensure a break from an era when Christianity was about anything but listening, but also to honor the great musical and preaching traditions of the Chapel as ways in which divine wisdom has long been shared and experienced. And it addressed in a non-sectarian way the person of God. In a subtle way this was designed to reiterate Augustine's point that without right worship there can be no true justice.[11] That's to say, as a Christian, I believe that unless

---

11. Augustine, *City of God*, trans. Henry Bettenson (London: Penguin, 2004), book 19.

we are listening to God there can be no flourishing of any life or institution. There is an important statement in the use of the term "listening" that stresses God as the true agent in all our life's endeavors and ourselves as simply small characters in a narrative whose protagonist has been fully disclosed in Jesus. But the phrase "listening to the heart" also, in a more popular way, spoke of a co-curricular role for the Chapel in addressing the heart of an institution that could otherwise tend to get a little too focused on its mind. As a whole, it said the Chapel's role was to be with God and to be with the institution in such way that inclined it to be with God too; which is a working definition of incarnational mission.

Another conclusion that arose from identifying the centrality of the undergraduate classroom was the role of student ministry. The Sunday morning worship service at Duke Chapel had a very large congregation. Around 600 would attend each Sunday during the breaks, rising to 900 on semester Sundays, with perhaps 1,200 on major Sundays, and maybe 4,000 at Christmas and Easter. And yet on regular semester Sundays there were seldom more than 50 or 100 undergraduates present. One could rejoice in the nearly twenty Christian campus ministries and simply assume students would find their way to something that suited them. But with the rapidly changing and diversifying demographic of students at Duke, that approach would doom the Chapel to becoming in the medium- to long-term a liturgical museum. I came to realize that the Chapel had to offer a vibrant student ministry of its own—one that made lively connections between faith, intellect, and worship.

And linked to this, I concluded that, if the heart of the university lay in the undergraduate classroom, that's where I needed to be. For my last four years I taught a course in the Public Policy school called "Ethics in an Unjust World," which looked at three models of social engagement. I called the course "Everything I was cross about when I was nineteen." Christianity played a significant but not dominant part in the course. At a university where the Religion Department doesn't approve of confessional teaching and the Divinity School is not routinely at liberty to teach undergraduates, this is one of the few chances undergraduates get to think seriously about engaging with poverty and addressing major social questions in ways that can challenge and stimulate their faith. I also hired colleagues who were qualified and able to teach undergraduates in similar areas such as religion and politics and interfaith partnerships.

Duke is in a unique geographical and cultural position because it's on the longitude of the Ivy League and on the latitude of the Bible belt. What that means is that it is an elite research university but that it's in a place where religion is almost always a legitimate part of the conversation. Duke's motto is the Latin phrase *Eruditio et Religio*. It comes from a line of a hymn written by Charles Wesley, which goes, "Unite the two so long disjoin'd, Knowledge and vital piety." What Wesley is talking about is the combination of faith and works, wisdom and service, knowing and doing. My role was to ensure that the Duke motto wasn't harking back to an outmoded notion of a Christian college but was a perennial and ever-new appeal to faculty, staff, and students, to make sure what they thought was never just words and ideas but became actions and relationships, and meanwhile what they did was never just activity, but was always material for reflection and analysis and better living. One way in which I sought to do this was to inaugurate a series known as the Dean's Dialogues, where two or three times a semester I interviewed a leading campus figure, usually the dean of a professional school, and quizzed the interviewees about what they were seeking to achieve, what challenges they were facing in their discipline, and how they saw the

future of university and society. Another way was to preach
sermons each Opening Sunday considering one aspect of the
university's life such as medicine or athletics or research or
science, and each Founders' Sunday considering the role of
faith and intellect and the new shibboleth, service.

When I became Dean of Duke Chapel I was aware of two
kinds of expectations. One was about an outmoded style of
ministry: that I would be fervently trying to drag Duke back
to an earlier era of Protestant cultural dominance. The other
was about a strident form of mission: that I would become a
self-styled champion of minority causes, often in a spirit of
working for, much as many chaplains were during the heyday
of the sixties. What instead I tried to do was to help Duke
become a model of what America in general and its universities in particular might seek to become; that is, a place where
it was assumed that everyone needed faith to live each day,
and what was interesting about meeting people different in
some respect from oneself was not getting cross about what
they didn't believe but becoming intrigued and fascinated
by what they did; a place where it was clear how respectfully
and generously faith enriched and broadened and deepened
the life of the intellect, and where it was equally obvious
how the life of the intellect challenged, refined, and in the
end strengthened faith. The most visible token of this philosophy was to establish a Faith Council made up of at least
one representative of each of the major global faiths and the
appointment of a Muslim (as well a Buddhist and a Hindu)
chaplain. There was an unspoken assumption inside and
outside the church that mainline Protestantism was doomed
and the job of someone in a role like mine was to hang on to
as much as I could for as long as I could. By saying I wanted
Duke to be as well known for its interfaith interaction as for
its Christian ministry, and that what's interesting and fruitful
about the faiths isn't what they have in common but where

they differ, I tried to suggest that the tasks and opportunities of the future might be different but just as rewarding as those of the past.

Duke faculty members live with the knowledge that, for all their remarkable research, outstanding teaching, and noted publications, their institution is primarily known locally as a hospital and nationally as a basketball team. The fact that the American healthcare system is riddled with anomalies, injustices, and compromises, and that NCAA sporting culture is swathed in suspicion, hypocrisy, and multiple standards, is known to all involved, insider and outsider alike, and frequently pointed out by academics such as members of the faculty at Duke. But both are the systems the nation's best efforts have arrived at to supply the need for healthcare and sporting aspiration. And thus they both provide fitting metaphors for the well-being of almost every visitor to the chair in my study, every one of whom is a mass of noble ideals, faltering endeavors, half-formed convictions, somewhat-articulated needs, divergent feelings, confused desires, and boundless capacity for self-deception.

For all that I've said about the advantages of formality, most conversations begin with small-talk. I therefore needed to be able to put people at their ease. Clergy invariably make people feel guilty, and judged, and foolish; thus everything I said in the first few moments of a pastoral encounter was designed to alleviate these anxieties, each of which seems in the North Carolina imagination to be exacerbated manifold by the presence of an educated Englishman. And so I was looking to express **delight**: to offer a simple compliment, to avoid passing an unsolicited negative opinion on anything, even the weather, and gently to divert attention from similarities or difference in status to the precious gift of this time now together. And that's exactly what I tried to do when I first took up my post. I won't deny that I easily tired of jokes about the UNC and Duke basketball rivalry, or a thousand other staples of daily conversation, but the point was to build the relationship and earn trust; and the only way to do that was to communicate the words, "I care about what you care about," as subtly and swiftly as possible. Needless to say, my visitor might be much better served by some more specialized help than I could give, and if that was the case it usually became obvious in these first few general remarks.

But when they were done, I wanted to go straight to the moment of truth. And I tended to be very direct. I'd say, "So, tell me all," or maybe, "When does the story begin?" or, if I was less sure why the person had come, something like, "How would you like to use the time?" Almost always the visitor would hesitate and say, "Oh, I don't know about all," or some such step backwards. But then, as gently as I could, I would try to reassure her that "all" was fine, which was really a way of encouraging the visitor to make the most of this opportunity to put into words her deepest anxieties and fears and hurts and regrets. This is the work of **attention**. And that's exactly what I tried to do when I started at Duke. Every time I've moved to a new post there's always been a crisis or event very early in my ministry that's made me wish I'd been there longer so that I'd know what to do or say. In each case, the relationships formed have been more important than what I did or said. Sure enough, at Duke in August 2005, three weeks after I first sat down in my office chair, it was Hurricane Katrina. Preaching about the event on Opening Sunday, I challenged the congregation to identify what this crisis had told them about nature, about America, about God, and about themselves. It was a bit like saying, "Tell me all." A few weeks later in my installation sermon I had a chance to reiterate the invitation, asking the congregation to locate their story in the story of Duke, the story of the south, the story of the American university, and the story of God.

Once the visitor had begun to articulate her story, her feelings, and her groping toward perception and insight, my pastoral role was then to be with her as she found words and wove together silences. She needed to know that she was not alone, that the painful things she said made me wince, that the terrible things she'd done saddened but didn't shock me, that the awful things she'd suffered grieved me, and that the unresolved situation she was in didn't make me rush in with a solution to fix it or a rapid remedy to settle it or a joke or a story to distract from or belittle it.

Unsurprisingly a great number of those who sat in the chair in the corner of my office told me that their story wasn't the Duke story of greatness building upon dizzying greatness. Everyone was obsessed with GPAs, or tenure, or whatever the symbol of success might be, but, inside, this person in the chair knew failure, and had profound fears, and wondered if she could keep up the pretense and play the public game anymore. And yet more than a little bit of this person craved and yearned for this culture of competition and striving and envy and accumulating she'd known all her life, otherwise she wouldn't have been there; because those were the energies that made the university swing. And that was my role at the university: to reflect back its glories and its absurdities, gently to bring its self-importance face to face with its private doubts and complex despairs, and generally to eye with skepticism its efforts to make itself immortal, while offering compassion on the occasions when it confronted its own mortality.

When my visitor reached the end of her story, I would try to demonstrate and check that I'd heard and understood by inviting my visitor to explore further and explain more fully. Like an osteopath or a chiropractor passing a gentle hand over a patient's back, I'd be stroking in one place and pushing in another, trying to find the tender area and see which movements made it worse and better. I would say, "I wonder which was your lowest moment in this whole saga," or, "I wonder what it's like to realize you don't come from a happy family," or, "Do you still dream about what happened?" What I'd be trying to do was to give permission to say the scariest, most embarrassing, shameful, or bitterly painful thing and then show that it's possible to live beyond it, outside it, around it, and then begin to face it down together and make a story that was not poisoned or dominated by it. I was still relatively new to the campus when (what turned out to be false) accusations were made against the lacrosse team in March 2006, but this was the role I thought it best to adopt. I shelved my prepared sermon for that Sunday and addressed a particularly large congregation without a script from the chancel steps, seeking to set a tone of vulnerability and shared ambiguity. I tried my best to articulate why this crisis was so troubling and how it could be a way of putting us in touch with the deepest values of the university to rediscover who we were as an institution. But what I was really trying to do was to dwell in the tender areas until the fear was faced. That's one of the most important roles I had at the university: to be a person who was not afraid to name what was really going on, and yet was able to do so without bitterness or rancor. Perhaps the most visible times this role was called upon was at moments of personal grief, such as the death and funeral of a student, or of public pain, such as after a shooting on a campus in the neighboring state that many knew well. These were extraordinary opportunities to dwell in places of heightened sensitivity and awareness and to model every element in the process I am describing. They were times when the **mystery** that bound the heart of the institution was most evident.

Then came the crucial moment in the pastoral conversation with my visitor. I would say, "Is that the whole story?" Of course it never was. I would stay silent for a while, to indicate it was okay to say more. That silence was the crucial moment in the whole conversation. It was a moment of hovering, a stretching-out of the hands and dwelling over the sensitive place—a moment that echoes the way, during a Eucharist, pastors hold out their arms over the bread and wine when asking the Holy Spirit to infuse these earthly elements with heavenly grace. It was an invitation to my visitor to go deeper, to go way down to the bottom of the pond if that's where the mystery lies and the pain resides. That's the gift every pastor needs more than almost anything else. That's what the pastor's people will remember—not the fine sermon or the marvelous fundraising program, but whether the pastor was willing and able to stare down to the bottom of that pond. And how can one demonstrate that on a campus? Only by being present in the unfashionable places at the unrewarded events and being willing to name and ask the uncomfortable things in ways that seek not exposure and humiliation but learning and understanding. Only by avoiding superficiality and false bonhomie and at every opportunity allowing others to say it's awful if it really is. You can't do this overnight. But when it's something people deeply want and have maybe never had before, they'll tell you. This is the fruit of **participation**.

And this was the point, the point where my visitor had named the elusive, incorrigible thing, where I would take a risk. I would listen to my gut and say what came. All the time I would be gauging permission from my visitor and saying only what I sensed she might be ready to hear. I would usually be doing one of two things.[12] One was to try to tell the person's story back to her in a way that highlighted how these

---

12. These two things I outline at length in my book *Improvisation: The Drama of Christian Ethics* (Grand Rapids: Brazos, 2004).

negative moments and incidents might resurface in her present or future in a form that could be somehow redemptive, or at least might not be wholly worthless and lost. That's reincorporation: when previously discarded elements reappear later in a story in ways that enable the story to continue. The other thing I would usually be doing was overaccepting. That means placing the person's own story within a much larger story, in relation to which the events of her story take on significantly different proportions and resonances. Rather than trying to suppress the sadness and disappointment, or simply resigning herself to it, my visitor was encouraged to see her portrait on a much larger canvas in which it could have much richer poignancy. The story might still be sad and painful, but reincorporation addressed the fear that all might be lost, while overaccepting addressed the additional anxiety that none of it really mattered. This was the way I sought to practice **enjoyment**.

These were the signal tasks I would take on when I preached sermons on major university occasions like Baccalaureate or led prayers on days like Convocation or Martin Luther King Day. I was trying to re-present the university's (and the society's) past, including its less savory flavors, and render it not a burden or a lie but a blessing and a gift. These were occasions when I had an opportunity to preach the gospel, even if it sometimes seemed inappropriate to use the word "Jesus." And this is how I understand salvation: Jesus takes our past, gives it back to us as a gift, and fits our tawdry story into his wondrous glory. Reincorporation and overaccepting—or, if you prefer, forgiveness and eternal life. In other words, the gospel.

The next moment in a pastoral visitation would be to seek to ensure the conversation ended on an empowering note, by inviting the visitor to craft some kind of plan of action based around this new insight that had emerged through the dialogue. This wasn't primarily to suggest there's a simple step to make anything better. It was more about ensuring the initiative lay with the visitor, and that she departed full of insight or resolve of her own, rather than dependent on whatever contribution I had made. On a campus level I sought to play this role by sitting on and chairing various university committees where the well-being of the university in its various dimensions could be discussed, representations made, recommendations offered, and policy ideas implemented. This was the element of **partnership**. I was glad not to have an executive role in the running of the university as a whole: working for would have jeopardized being with.

The penultimate activity in the visit might be the one most associated with the role of pastor. I usually ended a conversation with a person who had shown at least some inclination toward the Christian faith by offering to say a prayer. It may sound surprising, but I was slow to realize that modeling how to pray and relate to God by the way I led public prayers was one of the most important things I had the opportunity to do. In the prayer I was seeking to re-iterate the key elements of our conversation—the naming of the tender areas, the uttering of the unspeakable words, the hints of reincorporation, and the possibility of overaccepting. This was made infinitely easier by the witness of a lively and faithful Chapel, let alone a host of energetic and engaging campus ministries. I don't know how I could have done my job without constantly being able to point to a congregation and a body of students and colleagues whose lives showed what God could do. By inviting either an individual or the whole gathered university community to pray, I was ushering them into the company of worship, the angels and saints around the throne of grace, the constant enjoyment of God, and encouraging them to dwell, bask, and remain there. This was an experience of sharing **glory**. The gospel is toothless if there is no one you can point to who is living it.

And finally, every pastor knows the "door-handle moment." I learned not to put too much furniture near the door to my office, because a great many people would say the most important thing of all just as they were about to run away from the consequences of having said it, and others would discover why they had come only in the process of finding words to say thank you and goodbye. And so I needed to be prepared to stand by the door for long enough to establish whether this parting shot was truly a part of the conversation or not. And what that meant for being with the campus was to try to appear to be someone who was not in a hurry, who was not looking beyond each person I talked to for the more influential or attractive person behind him or her, who was able to enjoy the present tense and not see it as a trial run or a stepping stone or a résumé enhancement for what the future might hold.

This, in summary, is how I saw my ministry at Duke, as one instance of being with an institution. It was to dwell in places of encounter. It was to know myself and my people well enough that I had a reasonable understanding of the dynamic between us. It was to show people that I cared about what they cared about. It was to hover over the place of fear and tenderness long enough to know that pain and anxiety would not have the last word. It was to be comfortable with silence, and to listen to people's stories not just once but a second time, when they'd identified the parts that really mattered. It was to sit with them as they stared all the way to the bottom of the pond, tender and mysterious as the sight might be. It was to speak a word of truth, perhaps a word of hope, that reconfigured what had seemed to be unalterable givens, such that they might become gifts. It was to tell a larger story in which all our stories find their true context. It was to empower, and encourage, and watch people find their own futures. It was to pray and open out a world of worship and glory to each person I met. And it was not to rush, but to be still present even if the truth emerged only after the conversation was supposed to be over. Most of all, it was to do all of these with a whole community, a whole neighborhood, on high days and ordinary days, in sunshine, cloud, and rain.

CHAPTER 9

Being with Government

"The church stands neither absolutely *against* the state, nor does it stand always uncritically *for* the state, but it stands dialectically with the state."[1] This summary of Karl Barth's theological politics sets the agenda for what it means to be with government. To go further, "for Barth the Christian belongs to herself, the church, *and* the world. The Christian does not *choose* to be in solidarity with the world, says Barth, but 'is in solidarity with it from the very first.'"[2]

We may note here that, rather than simply being contrasted with the preposition for, in this case with stands as a mean between the two extremes of "for" (in the sense of in favor of, rather than the usual on behalf of) and "against." The key term that places both church and state in their correct respective roles is "kingdom." Both church and state serve kingdom. The church goes awry in a number of possible

1. David Haddorff, in Karl Barth, *Community, State and Church: Three Essays*, with an introduction by Will Herberg and a new introduction by David Haddorff (Eugene: Wipf and Stock, 2004), xxxix, italics original.

2. Haddorff, in Barth, *Community, State and Church*, l, italics original; citing Karl Barth, *Church Dogmatics*, IV/4: *The Christian Life*, trans. Geoffrey W. Bromiley (Edinburgh: T & T Clark, 2004), 194.

ways: by paying uncritical homage to the state, by assuming a lofty yet superior distance from the state, by presuming the state's principal purpose is to advance or privilege the church, or by becoming the state.

To change the prepositions, one could call the church's two possible mistakes as to be "above" or "under" the state. Barth points out that both are misguided forms of self-preservation. To be under the state—to have insufficient critical distance from the world's ideologies—is to become what Barth calls a "secular church." The mistake here is to forget that "the Christian community has a task of which the civil community can never relieve it and which it can never pursue in the forms peculiar to the civil community.... It proclaims the rule of Jesus Christ and the hope of the Kingdom of God."[3]

By contrast, the "sacral church" is overconfident in its knowledge of God and its status as sole bearer of God's truth: it ends up using God and enjoying only itself, becoming confused about its mission, incapable of hearing God's word of judgment on itself, and mistaking itself for the kingdom. This can lead to it isolating itself, becoming antagonistic toward the worldly other, and incapable of hearing the secular parables at large in the world.

There is indeed a proper role, in God's reign, for the state. Writing in 1946, in the wake of the Nazi catastrophe, Barth argues:

> However much human error and human tyranny may be involved in it, the State is not a product of sin but ... an instrument of divine grace ... inasmuch as ... in relation to the world that still needs redeeming, the grace of God

---

3. Karl Barth, "The Christian Community and Civil Community," in Barth, *Community, State and Church*, 157–58.

is always the patience of God.... It is outside the Church
but not outside the range of Christ's dominion—it is an
exponent of His Kingdom. The activity of the State is ... a
form of divine service.... The Church can in no case be indifferent or neutral towards this manifestation of an order
so clearly related to its own mission.[4]

Accordingly, in his Ethics, Barth suggests the state "is the sign,
set up by God's revelation, of the concrete and visible order of
life by which and in which, on the basis of accomplished reconciliation, we are summoned to serve our neighbor."[5] "Both
church and state remain committed to peace and justice, in a
world that is 'not yet redeemed.' The state is not completely
governed by autonomous devilish principles of power and
force, and the church by merciful spiritual principles of love
and hope."[6] Thus the church should neither eulogize nor con-
demn the state.

For Barth, a proper state balances order, freedom, community, power, and responsibility in equal proportions; none
is allowed to overshadow the others. One that does so can become an allegory of the kingdom of God.[7] In this context the
church's own task becomes easier to elucidate. Its role is to
witness to Christ, primarily through preaching, teaching, and
administering the sacraments, and to remind the state of its
need to repent and its ability to advance justice and peace. Its
role is not to advance its own privileges or demand that the
state defend its own causes. Instead it advances humanity's
causes. For Barth, these include constitutional democracy, social and economic justice, basic human rights, political equality, equal protection of all citizens under the law, and the right

4. Barth, "The Christian Community and Civil Community," 156.
5. Karl Barth, Ethics (New York: Seabury, 1981), 445.
6. Haddorff, in Barth, Community, State and Church, xxiv–xxv.
7. Barth, "The Christian Community and Civil Community," 169.

to engage in civil society through family, education, art, science, religion, and culture.[8] Those from a common-good tradition might summarize these as a stable political, legal, economic, and cultural order.[9] Where Barth is adamant is that the church has no business establishing or wholly endorsing a political party. "There can be no such thing as a Christian state or Christian political party. The church cannot promote a particular form of government or party to the exclusion of others, without seeking to be itself the state."[10] Instead, political responsibility is "taking that human initiative which the State cannot take; it is giving the State the impulse which it cannot give itself; it is reminding the State of those things of which it is unable to remind itself."[11]

Barth sees twelve analogies between the church's role and the state's role—each of which is predicated on the incarnation: just as in the incarnate Christ God stands with humanity, so in various ways the church stands with the civil community. The church witnesses to God's justification, so governments uphold impartial justice. Christ came to the lost, so the state supports the poor. God gave freedom, so church and state resist totalitarianism. As the church is a community of individuals, so the state avoids political individualism and collectivism. As baptism offers equality to the faithful, so politics seeks equality among citizens. Spiritual gifts are diverse but necessary, so powers in government are separated but each required. As God's word is freely proclaimed, so the state guarantees freedom of speech. And so on.[12]

8. As summarized by Haddorff, in Barth, *Community, State and Church*, xlii.

9. See Patrick Riordan, SJ, "Aristotle and the Politics of Common Good Today," in *Together for a Common Good: Towards a National Conversation*, ed. Nicholas Sagovsky and Peter McGrail (London: SCM, 2015), 45.

10. Haddorff, in Karl Barth, *Community, State and Church*, xxxix.

11. Barth, "The Christian Community and Civil Community," 170.

12. Barth, "The Christian Community and Civil Community," 172–79.

Before moving from the state and civil society in general to government in particular, we need to examine one word a little more closely: "politics." Politics can mean three broad, somewhat overlapping things. It most commonly refers to the adversarial relationship between the government—in a constitutional democracy, the party with the most representatives in the elected legislature—and the minority parties, over great issues like justice and punishment, defense, health, education, employment, welfare, and external relations, and the budgetary and presentational dimensions and balance of priorities among them. Into this culture comes the cult of personality, the short-term orientation to opinion polls and electoral appeal, the jockeying among governing party aficionados, and the frequent frustration and exasperation that principle and wisdom are being sacrificed to expediency and appearance.

But politics can more broadly mean, second, healthy consensus based on the necessary foundation of the rule of law, recognition of the inevitability and indispensability of conflict, and acceptance of and respect for the structures and disciplines of representative democracy.

A third notion of politics is broader still and indicates wider engagement in associational, organizational, and institutional life. It recognizes that to build anything socially or to change something communal for the better involves bringing together coalitions of interest, constructing networks of support, using influence to gain the attention of those in control, developing grassroots power, discerning where compromises must be made, distinguishing between long-term and short-term goals, forming a communications strategy, securing sources of income, rewarding and motivating supporters, gaining momentum, inspiring a team, making difficult choices, negotiating with diverse stakeholders, facing criticism and hostility, and recovering from setbacks. Those who cannot or will not engage in such habits are unlikely to succeed and will need to find contentment in such projects as can flourish in isolation.

All three of these dimensions of politics are at work when the church seeks to be with the civil community. But there yet lies one further set of distinctions that benefit those who seek to engage with government—and those are the differences between the conventional notions of politics outlined above and what Aristotle believed constituted political discourse.[13] Aristotle assumed a political community had a shared notion of good and evil, right and wrong, just and unjust. Likewise he took for granted that, as in his view all action was for some good, so all collaboration was intended for something thought to be good—although that good was not always the same. Thus he began from a projection of shared moral vision and social harmony, where legislators sought to enhance the goodness of citizens and aspired to the very best in human potential. By contrast, politics today assumes diversity of identity and vision and takes for granted that such diversity creates conflict. Rather than identify or impose any account of the good, politicians applaud liberty and enforce only compliance to a minimum—that minimum being usually considered to involve harm to others and to be articulated in rights, those being what an individual can expect no other person or the state to do to him or her.

How the church can engage in politics without that politics having a shared notion of the good, attention to the formation of character, or final goal to which all aspire constitutes the key question of what it means to be with government. For government names the process by which in a political system a set of people become assigned to set policy and institute that policy through legislation, being periodi-

13. This paragraph follows the analysis in Riordan, "Aristotle and the Politics of Common Good Today," 36–46.

cally accountable to the electorate for what they have done and propose henceforth to do; but government also names the reality that most authority and power are gained and exercised in responding to events, rather than in determining them, and that those seen as powerful by others are often largely aware of their limitations and the way their authority is circumscribed. In what follows I explore what the hopes of Aristotle and the wisdom of Karl Barth bring to the practice of relating to government.

John F. Kennedy's words from his inaugural address, "My fellow Americans: ask not what your country can do for you; ask what you can do for your country," set an agenda for being with government. For they break the assumption that the office of government is a privilege for its members, the cost of which is that they become subject to unceasing, partial, and increasingly irascible demands. Jesus's parable of the persistent widow depicts a world where only constant petition elicits results.

> In a certain city there was a judge who neither feared God nor had respect for people. In that city there was a widow who kept coming to him and saying, "Grant me justice against my opponent." For a while he refused; but later he said to himself, "Though I have no fear of God and no respect for anyone, yet because this widow keeps bothering me, I will grant her justice, so that she may not wear me out by continually coming." (Luke 18:2–5)

This is a parable of **presence** as well as persistence. It echoes the scene in which Hannah repeatedly cries out to God and pleads that she may be given her heart's desire.

> Hannah rose and presented herself before the Lord.... She was deeply distressed and prayed to the Lord, and wept

bitterly.... As she continued praying before the Lord, Eli observed her mouth. Hannah was praying silently; only her lips moved, but her voice was not heard; therefore Eli thought she was drunk. So Eli said to her, "How long will you make a drunken spectacle of yourself? Put away your wine." But Hannah answered, "No, my lord, I am a woman deeply troubled; I have drunk neither wine nor strong drink, but I have been pouring out my soul before the Lord. Do not regard your servant as a worthless woman, for I have been speaking out of my great anxiety and vexation all this time." Then Eli answered, "Go in peace; the God of Israel grant the petition you have made to him." ... Elkanah knew his wife Hannah, and the Lord remembered her. (1 Sam. 1:9–19)

These passages highlight a number of features of political engagement: the ability to cope with hostility, indifference, and misunderstanding; the willingness to make connections with gatekeepers of power; resolute tenacity in the face of discouragement; an ability to turn weakness to one's own advantage; and a clear sense of what constitutes success. But more importantly, for our purposes, is the estimation of the value of physical presence. These are not messages sent from afar, petitions submitted through the usual channels, frustrations aired to sympathetic audiences; this is in-your-face encounter, relentless determination, unwavering concentration on the target to be addressed. This is how Jesus suggests disciples intercede; this therefore becomes their model for any relationship where there is an imbalance of power and the one with the greater power is withholding something precious, honored, and loved.

Presence in politics can mean "I am not going away"; it can indicate "I am watching you"; or it can denote "I am by your side." After the murder of the Batley and Spen MP, Jo Cox, in Birstall, West Yorkshire, in June 2016, days before the

Brexit vote, a number of gatherings were arranged. One of them attracted thousands in Trafalgar Square, London, on her birthday, June 20. It recalled words from her maiden speech in Parliament a year previously, "We are far more united and have far more in common than that which divides us," and affirmed her conviction that "love is stronger than hate, unity is stronger than division, hope is stronger than fear." This was a tender but public way of saying "I am by your side"—a determination, in the words of famous speakers at the occasion, to "Love like Jo." One mourner described the meaning of her presence in these words:

> If we are to honour Jo and create a lasting legacy for her work, let it be in our social justice campaigning; tirelessly speaking up for humanity with a fierce compassion and generosity; let it be in how we disagree with humility, a listening ear and an open heart. Let it be in how we relate to those in power; believing the good before the bad, congratulating our leaders when they do well and supporting them when they fail.
>
> Let it be in how we look at the "other" in the face; the stranger, the foreigner, the one with a different accent or who holds a different political view from our own—looking for the common humanity before the difference, and seeking to make friends rather than enemies.[14]

Such words turn the passion of Hannah and the persistent widow into the selfless solidarity of the common good in a more Aristotelian practice of politics despite the challenges of diversity and conflict.

---

14. Katherine Maxwell-Rose, "More in Common: Celebrating the Life of Jo Cox," *Tearfund Lifestyle*, June 20, 2016, https://lifestyle.tearfund .org/article/more-in-common-celebrating-the-life-of-jo-cox/.

Being present in the sense of "I am watching you" is the spirit of the School of the Americas Watch. In 1990 former Maryknoll Father Roy Bourgeois founded an advocacy organization to highlight and draw attention to the training of Latin American military officers by the United States Department of Defense, at a location near Columbus, Georgia, since 2000 known as the Western Hemisphere Institute for Security Cooperation.[15] Bourgeois and members of the Watch hold the institution responsible for the countless acts of murder, rape, and torture and contraventions of the Geneva Conventions perpetrated by graduates of the so-called school. The Watch cites incidents such as the 1980 assassination of Archbishop Oscar Romero and the 1989 murders of six Jesuit priests, their housekeeper, and her daughter at the Central American University in El Salvador as examples of the atrocities that US personnel trained Latin American students to carry out. The Watch holds an annual November protest to mark the anniversary of the Jesuit killings. What began as a protest of ten people has become a gathering of ten thousand. While this might be regarded as working for the oppressed of Latin America, it's perhaps better identified as being with the US Government, over a period of more than twenty-five years, and, as Barth puts it, "reminding the State of those things of which it is unable to remind itself."

But presence is not limited to gestures of concern, solidarity, or patience in the face of adversity. It can involve a more positive practice of being with government—"showing up." When I used to teach a class in a university school of public policy I would arrange for the students to visit either a school board or a city council meeting for an evening. Besides being challenged by the degree of detail and the emphasis on due procedure, the students' strongest reactions had to do

15. See http://www.soaw.org/about-us.

with the care and concern for the well-being of the city and its residents and the extent to which all this was carried out largely without any engagement from the population whose democracy and rights were so frequently extolled. As we have seen, showing up can be a form of scrutiny or protest that is anything but affirmation; but any affirmation or gratitude for the selflessness and service of those who seek the welfare of the city on the citizens' behalf is inadequate if it doesn't in some measure involve showing up.

Moving to **attention**, it's important to recognize, with Karl Barth, that being with government is highly dependent on context. What may be necessary and appropriate in one context may equally be foolish and misguided in another. Consider the oft-controversial question of the payment of taxes. A position that claims to establish what being government might mean in all circumstances would be misguided because in practice it would privilege the social context of the person proposing it. But the joy of being a disciple is that there are disciples in all circumstances in all places in the world. The account of the question posed to Jesus, "Is it lawful to pay taxes to the emperor, or not?," is intended not to have a definitive context, but to offer a definitive approach: "Give therefore to the emperor the things that are the emperor's, and to God the things that are God's" (Matt. 22:17, 22). What does this approach mean? Let me suggest five social contexts and propose what might be an appropriate attitude to taxation in each one.

1. **Minority community under an oppressive regime.** This is the original context of Jesus's exchange. The interlocutors are three: (1) the Herodians, quislings of the Romans, happy to do the dirty work for the regime and skim off some of the profits while nominally preserving a puppet Jewish presence in positions of power; (2) the Pharisees, more given to pursuing holiness for the Jewish people as a whole and

less inclined to join or disturb the Roman-dominated political status quo; and (3) Jesus, apparently set on transforming both the political and the religious establishment by accepting the titles Son of David and Son of God. Under an oppressive regime, Jesus's answer, "Give to the emperor the things that are the emperor's, and to God the things that are God's," is ironic: it highlights that, in a world where the Roman emperor thinks everything is his, Jesus holds that everything is God's. Nothing can be the emperor's without being first and always God's too. So for Christians to pay taxes is not a grudging, resentful recognition that they have no choice but a hopeful epiphany of God's sovereignty and a statement that, though the emperor might mean it for evil, God doubtless will mean it for good. Don't let the fear of Caesar obscure the wonder of God.

2. **A minority community in a "failed" state or in circumstances where conventional law and order is in abeyance or has broken down.** To ignore this context is to fail to understand how Christian political theology took shape. Political chaos is not the reign of God. Contemporary Syria and Yemen are not easy places to find or express love, joy, peace, and the rest. In such contexts the irony of Jesus's comments is largely lost; instead what remains is the conviction that Christians do have a stake in and a duty to be with the state, not just to give it space to be the church but because, without a minimum of order, few things of value in God's creation can flourish. These are perhaps the only circumstances in which Luther's two-kingdoms notion—wherein God functions right-handedly through grace and the church and left-handedly through law and the state—needs a greater hearing. Don't let rendering to God make you forget Caesar altogether.

3. **A minority community under a regime that is not oppressing the community but that the community believes**

to be oppressing other social groups or nations. This is what might be called the activist view of America—a view that sees the federal government through the lens of the School of the Americas. Jesus's words become especially significant if one attempts to calculate the percentage of one's taxes that will be used, say, on nuclear weapons and to work out a way of withholding that percentage. This maintains the ironic dimension of Jesus's words by perceiving the majority of one's tax contribution as "giving to God" but assuming that funding nuclear weapons could never be regarded as a gift to God. This approach puts a very high value on keeping a clean individual conscience but puts a low value on trusting the organic deliberative role of the state and its officers. Don't let faith in God make you lose all faith in Caesar.

4. A nominally majority community with access to a regime that sees itself as having a divine mandate. What the activists see is really there—but the wider context is not so much the bureaucratic cynicism that says "no one can stop us" as the misplaced governmental sense of vocation that says "America must do this for the sake of its own freedom and the freedom of the world (which are, of course, indistinguishable, not just in the long term but in the immediate term)." The curious thing is that the rhetoric of this context sounds suspiciously similar to the language of (2) above—i.e., "Only a strong America prevents the world lapsing into chaos." But this rhetoric invites citizens to buy into a divine (or at least salvific) mission that has to be named as no less than idolatry. And so here again the ironic note of Jesus's appeal to what is owed to God is vital. Service to America is not identical to service to God. Loyalty to one's place of birth and ties of national belonging are healthy but limited; loyalty to God is absolute. To get them mixed up is idolatry. This is what Barth means when he says, "the fulfillment of political duty means rather responsible choices of authority,

responsible decision about the validity of laws, responsible care for their maintenance, in a word, political action, which may also mean political struggle," for "there is no cause for the Church to act as though it lived, in relation to the State, in a night in which all cats are grey."[16] Don't let rendering to Caesar stop you rendering to God.

5. **A minority presence in an ordered state, where the state has limited notions of its ability to carry out a noble mission.** It's foolish to think in terms of an ideal state in which to be a Christian, but this would seem better than most. If a state is well-ordered but open to constructive contributions and friendly criticism from Christians and the church, then it seems possible to imagine some of the irony of Jesus's words being withdrawn. Then rendering to Caesar is an aspect of, but by no means a substitute for or a displacement from, rendering to God. When taxes are the principal form of discipleship, the state has become too much; when taxes are almost incompatible with discipleship, the state has become too little. Christians' anxiety that the state shouldn't exceed its brief shouldn't blind them to what only the state can legitimately or efficiently do. When Christians seek the welfare of the city, but also the city that is to come, taxes should be a statement of common humanity and collective trust: a form of ordinary rendition.

This is the kind of detailed attention that is required for being with government. It also discloses a level of **mystery**. Mystery names the journey from the functional and utilitarian view of government as the fixer of problems and the arbitrator of competing interests to the more Aristotelian view of politics as that which pursues a shared vision with the end of enhancing character and approximating final human purposes. Mystery most evidently resides in the symbols and

16. Barth, "Church and State," in *Community, State and Church,* 144, 119.

rituals that pervade legislative assemblies; in the reverence for such items as the American flag and the US Constitution, or the crown jewels, regalia, and vestments that the British monarch wears at the State Opening of Parliament; and in the almost sacramental application of a cross to a ballot paper—the act that most explicitly embodies democracy.

In more general terms mystery means appreciation for the existence of peaceable government, transition of power, and the rule of law—the groundwork of well-functioning political structures. It recognizes that government is not simply a means to an end, but a display of what a society values, respects, and honors. When, as in the case of Jo Cox, a representative is murdered, it is mystery that articulates why such an act is an attack upon democracy itself. Mystery elucidates the dignity of political office, the way it is held in trust and passed to the next occupant, the manner in which a duty to the public transcends political persuasion or party affiliation. Being with government in an attitude of mystery is exactly, again employing Barth's words quoted earlier, "taking that human initiative which the State cannot take; it is giving the State the impulse which it cannot give itself; it is reminding the State of those things of which it is unable to remind itself."[17]

Margaret Thatcher voiced this same sense of mystery when she entered 10 Downing Street for the first time as Prime Minister in May 1979. She said,

> Her Majesty The Queen has asked me to form a new administration and I have accepted. It is, of course, the greatest honor that can come to any citizen in a democracy. I know full well the responsibilities that await me as I enter the door of Number 10 and I'll strive unceasingly to try to fulfil the trust and confidence that the British people

17. Barth, "The Christian Community and Civil Community," 170.

have placed in me and the things in which I believe. And I would just like to remember some words of St Francis of Assisi which I think are really just particularly apt at the moment. "Where there is discord, may we bring harmony. Where there is error, may we bring truth. Where there is doubt, may we bring faith. And where there is despair, may we bring hope." And to all the British people—howsoever they voted—may I say this. Now that the Election is over, may we get together and strive to serve and strengthen the country of which we're so proud to be a part.[18]

In doing so she set a standard by which her administration may be judged. Mystery can include holding leaders to accounts of the texture of authority to which they appeal. Such was the role of being with government when it came to reminding the Prime Minister of her words, "Where there is discord, may we bring harmony," in the light of the miners' strike of 1984; of her words, "Where there is error, may we bring truth," in the light of the sinking of the *General Belgrano* as it sailed out of the exclusion zone around the Falkland Islands in 1982; of her words, "Where there is doubt, may we bring faith," in the light of her minister's denunciation of the Archbishop of Canterbury's Commission on Urban Priority Areas' 1985 *Faith in the City* report as "pure Marxist theology"; of her words, "Where there is despair, may we bring hope," in the light of the Liverpool riots of 1981 and 1985.

In relation to government, **delight** does not have to mean neglecting its inherent witness to the state, or rejoicing in the pretensions of government to the extent of losing its critical distance. But it does mean, along with **participation**,

18. Margaret Thatcher, "Remarks on Becoming Prime Minister (St Francis's Prayer)," May 4, 1979. Accessed at http://www.margaret thatcher.org/document/104078.

developing a constructive and engaged account of political involvement, rather than assuming the limit of encounter is speaking truth to power (where the power belongs entirely to others, and truth adheres wholly to oneself). This has to begin with a celebration of the quality of interactive life available in liberal democracies and the unique location of the churches to capitalize on their social location. Thus the community organizer Ed Chambers identifies seven reasons why churches make promising bases for broad-based organizing.

- They invariably own a building with a presentation area and a dialogue area, breakout spaces and kitchen facilities.
- They have at least one full- or part-time person trained in leadership development, in governance, oversight, and practical ministry roles.
- They have a fundraising system, for internal expenses and external donations.
- They have a network of volunteers who offer their time, experience, skills, and personal connections.
- They have grassroots membership and deep knowledge of, and respect from, their communities. They are among very few places where different socioeconomic groups regularly and enthusiastically interact.
- They are concerned for and talk about the well-being of their communities.
- And they are comfortable with (at least their own language of) values, vision, and goals.[19]

One study identified four gifts that congregations bring to community resilience: a sense that all are connected and

19. This is my own distillation of a summary of Ed Chambers's observations provided by Cameron Harder, *Discovering the Other: Asset-Based Approaches for Building Community Together* (Lanham, MD: Rowman and Littlefield, 2013), 68–71.

called to serve one another (leading to volunteering); rituals that help communities process change, notably coming-of-age and grieving; a sense of coherence or meaning that enables communities to hope; and perception of a wider spectrum of wealth than simply money, commodities, and educated people.[20]

Based on these advantages, the practice of appreciative inquiry offers one model to energize and mobilize local churches and their civil neighborhoods. It seeks to enable people to see God at work in their past, imagine a future of possibility with God, and work together in the present to shape a godly community. It is an attempt to instill aspirational Aristotelian notions of politics amid contemporary minimal assumptions. Thus it doesn't look like conventional politics but fosters soil in which a better, more empowered politics can grow—a politics that is less passive and negative. It employs four kinds of positive questions.

- Peak experience: what has been good, and of God, in our past—notably acts of courage taken together, a time when you changed because you listened, or a time when others benefited because you were part of making a decision.
- Core values: what you most value about your community—about its young people, its open spaces, its history.
- Hope: what you long for—and how things would be different were those wishes to come true.
- Commitments: what you would be willing to offer to make those wishes come true. This involves asset-mapping.[21]

---

20. University of Queensland study, *Building Resilience in Rural Communities*, quoted in Cameron Harder, *Discovering the Other*, 121–22.

21. Harder, *Discovering the Other*, 83–87, building on David Cooperrider, Peter Sorenson Jr., Diana Whitney, and Therese Yaeger, *Appreciative*

Asset-mapping is a way of enabling a community to establish its often-unarticulated resources so as to perceive patterns and connect initiatives and thus release power. It recognizes that innovation largely arises from making connections between elements not previously linked. It assumes that "breadth of experience, intelligence, information and energies represented in a population far exceed that which the community system takes into account."[22] A simple but vivid example goes like this. A congregation discovered that

> in their large town a lot of seniors had extra space in their homes and wanted someone to live with them. Having a housemate made the seniors feel secure, because their health was frail or unpredictable. At the same time the community had an influx of young, mainly single oil-industry related workers who couldn't find housing. In response, a group from the congregation and community developed a Home Share program that matched (and screened) seniors who had rooms with newcomers who needed housing and had companionship and home maintenance skills to offer. The program was so successful that the provincial government picked it up.[23]

Among guidelines for asset-mapping, the following stand out: encouraging those who generate an idea to carry it out; keeping projects small by restricting the design and implementation to the same group of people; and judging projects

---

Enquiry: Rethinking Human Organization toward a Positive Theory of Change (Champaign, IL: Stipes, 1999).

22. James B. Cook, "Community Development Theory," quoted in Harder, *Discovering the Other*, 112.

23. Harder, *Discovering the Other*, 111.

as a way of building people, rather than perceiving people as useful for achieving the project.[24]

Such is the essence of delight, which sees abundance where most see only scarcity, even in themselves, and participation, which trusts in the significance of being with for its own sake rather for some extraneous goal to which it is an apt means.

Even though Barth is writing in the midst of painful relationships between church and government—spineless capitulation of the church, as he saw it, in the form of the German Christians, and sacrificial witness against the state, on the part of the Confessing Church—still he assumes that the church's relationship with government is fundamentally and normally one of **partnership**. Church and government each do things the other cannot (or should not try to) do; and both can be instruments of God's peace. The government must give the church freedom to exercise its ministry of calling people to be reconciled with God and one another, and the church must respect the government's role in seeking prosperity and human flourishing grounded in the rule of law and social order, even when the government's policies are not those the church itself would choose.

Being with various levels of government is to a significant degree about partnership. Partnership means understanding and respecting what another body can and should do, establishing and articulating what the church or a local congregation can and should do, and developing a healthy, supportive, enriching, and appropriately challenging relationship between the two bodies, often involving other bodies sooner or later. The joy of partnership is that it is not one body simply acting for or toward another body, but both bodies acting together, each bringing their distinct and char-

24. Harder, *Discovering the Other*, 129–33.

acteristic capabilities and making the most of their unique and timely opportunities.

There is no template for such partnerships: a great deal depends on the social situation and the political and economic circumstances. Thus under an oppressive regime the church's relationship with the government can still be a partnership, but it is one in which the church's role includes a greater share of challenge and calling the government to account. In a more benign political climate, the church's network of congregations dispersed across a country may play a major role in the delivery of healthcare to an underserved population or provide meeting spaces for programs for children in basic education or for adults in AIDS awareness or lessons in public hygiene. In a struggling economic culture, a congregation may partner with a local business to provide start-up units for entrepreneurs to get a foothold and provide employment; in a more healthy economic season the same congregation may look to foster social enterprises that have a wider community benefit than the bottom line and, for example, seek to employ and rehabilitate ex-offenders or to offer advantageous opportunities for people who use wheelchairs. Likewise, in a relatively stable social setting a congregation engaged with issues in civil society may work with a variety of other institutions to offer lively and family-friendly holiday activities for school-age children in a neighborhood; while in a more troubled community the church may convene a diverse collection of faith groups, voluntary associations, and informal networks to address a breakdown of relations between local young people and the police.

In partnership a congregation recognizes its responsibilities as a good neighbor and its opportunities as a people with a view of the past shaped by forgiveness and an understanding of the future liberated by eternal life. These are its primary opportunities to witness, but that witness will invariably be more about actions than words if it is to show appropriate attention, mystery, delight, and enjoyment. That sense of respect is evident in the way the congregation prays. Prayer in the context of partnership is largely about thanksgiving and intercession. By entering into partnerships readily and eagerly rather than hesitatingly, grudgingly, or suspiciously, a congregation shows its gratitude that God has surrounded it with everything it needs to discover the kingdom in its neighborhood. Like Joash seeing the sickness of Elisha, the local congregation says, "My father, my father! The chariots of Israel and its horsemen!" (2 Kings 13:14), seeing not the scarcity of its situation but the abundance of what God has given it. But just as partnership is the definitive place where the congregation and the disciple find their respective roles in relation to God, so partnership becomes the place where a congregation learns how the Holy Spirit acts through agencies other than the church. Like every act of intercession, it takes the risk of discovering that God may answer the prayer, and the outcome may be wonderful, but the way of answering the prayer may be different from that anticipated and the channel of that outcome may be one that humbles the intercessor, particularly the one that says, "Can anything good come out of Nazareth?" (John 1:46).

In practice, partnership can be of two kinds. The first refers to legislative activity. Lord Palmerston believed it was not necessary or possible to go on adding to the statute book forever, but subsequent governments have been inclined to disagree. While it's not the church's role to initiate or devise legislation, neither is it appropriate to confine one's perspective merely to opposing aspects one finds objectionable. This is where Barth's language of prototype is helpful. He says,

> The real Church must be the model prototype for the real State. The Church must set an example so that by its very

existence it may be a source of renewal for the State.... The Church's preaching of the gospel would be in vain if its own existence, constitution, order, government and administration were not a practical demonstration of thinking and acting from the gospel.[25]

Here what I have described as the activities of delight and participation contribute to making the church a community whose practical wisdom and lived examples provide concrete testimony to legislators of good ways to live. It is not that the church is constantly reactive, waiting for government to initiate proposals that it may then find disappointing and unsatisfactory; nor is it that the church constantly issues blueprints for social reform, taking to itself the mantle of policy-making; it is that the church relentlessly generates forms of social relating that address the isolation that's at the root of most human deprivation and that encourage the collaboration that's the source of most human flourishing. When church leaders speak publicly on a given issue, their authority for doing so lies not in some universally recognized spiritual credibility (for, rightly or wrongly, there is none) but, in large part, in the fact that they bring into the debate a host of local initiatives and historic endeavors that constitute a great reservoir of engagement, investment, and discovery of how being with people can help them bring out the best in themselves.

The second kind of partnership arises when the government perceives local congregations or parachurch agencies as the most propitious mechanisms for delivering public services. In an era when the fashion is to reduce government spending, and when at the same time many churches are both increasingly aware of their ability to meet God in the

25. Barth, "The Christian Community and Civil Community," 186.

neediest in their neighborhoods and yet anxious about their sustainability, government-funded faith-based initiatives are common. If local congregations have the knowledge of and respect from their civil communities, why not use that to good effect? Secular voices are often heard expressing caution that churches may use such opportunities to proselytize. More of a danger is that churches become so submerged in delivering the state's requirements and agenda that they lose the ability to be what only churches can be. This is a point where careful discernment is needed and generalized judgments are unhelpful. It constitutes a key area of partnership between church and government; but it offers ready evidence of the pitfalls of being too eager to practice working with when sometimes being with is preferable.

It is taken for granted in most circles, sacred and secular, that government is for use rather than for **enjoyment**. There seems an almost universal assumption that everyone—the voter, the lobbyist, the taxpayer, the party devotee, and the disciple—can get more out of politics in general and government in particular than they put into it. It's considered appropriate to look upon the activities of government with cynicism and disdain—at best to examine them like customers checking a purchase and a bill to be reassured they have not received damaged goods or been ripped off. And yet when politicians themselves take the same attitude and are judged to have taken more than they have given, the public are horrified. An attitude of use rather than enjoyment is corrosive. Clearly there are a great many jobs that only government can do, and consequently must do; but there must be a quality of government that is not simply regarded as a more or less efficient way of getting these jobs done. This is, as I noted at the outset, a more Aristotelian perspective: that representative democracy and its processes are a good in themselves, beyond what goods they may achieve and secure on behalf of voters. Politics is not fundamentally the flawed division of scarce resources to unsatisfied consumers; it is more significantly the harnessing of the full energies, talents, resources, and commitments of a people for that people's best flourishing.

To be with government in this spirit is best exercised by supportive, cordial, and engaged relationships with legislators on all levels, from the most humble to the most exalted. It has often been thought that the role of the chaplain in such a context was to whisper in the ear of the governor, "You are dust." But perhaps more important than reminding the powerful of their mortality and the prospect of their future judgment is to affirm them in the responsibility they carry—not so as to secure some privilege or advantage from them but simply to encourage them to aspire to be worthy of the high calling to which they have been elevated. To enjoy high office is to exercise its powers and possibilities to the fullest degree; to use high office is to forget its real power and take the opportunity to buy favor, show partiality, strip its moral assets, and enhance personal gain. Limitations on periods of office are a reminder that such a calling is a privilege and can never become an entitlement, however successful or worthy the service rendered therein. Being with government in a spirit of enjoyment is thus less asking, "Have you become obsessed with your own shadow and intoxicated by power?" than it is to inquire, "Are you employing the full range of influence and authority at your disposal to exercise your powers to the fullest and achieve the best balance between governing by enforcing and circumscribing and governing by empowering and permitting?"

And this challenges a conventional notion of **glory**. For a worldly notion of glory is surely what Margaret Thatcher felt when, puffed up with victory at the polls and with the delight of her party, she stood at the threshold of Prime Ministerial majesty. When people seek the highest office, is it truly because they want to carry out an extensive policy and legislative program—or simply because they want to be the one behind the largest desk, to occupy the location where the buck finally stops? But being with government is not primarily about this kind of glory. It's about recognizing the inextricable relationship between being with and the quality of trust. For trust is the tender, fragile, yet indispensable, essential, integral, and ultimately glorious form that being with takes when it means allowing another to attend to do what one cannot do alone. Glory is, finally, what it means for God to give humble and flawed humanity the privilege of sharing in the divine presence, of coinciding with the divine will, of beholding the divine countenance. And when one knows that God's unique and overarching will has been exercised through one's own fitful actions, one gets a glimpse of the frisson, delight, and enjoyment of that glory. Government gives glimpses and intimations of what it means to bring presence, attention, mystery, and the rest all together in one carefully discerned act of faithful service. And that is why being with government can offer opportunities to inhabit that glory.

CHAPTER 10

Being with the Excluded

In the second half of this book we have considered people in social terms. We began with organizations, corporate bodies through which people aggregate to earn a living and to which people are drawn to furnish the necessities of life. These are mostly commercial, although in some societies some organizations are resourced in other ways. Then we moved to institutions, those forms of civil society through which citizens organize themselves to enrich their lives and the lives of others politically, culturally, or socially. And then there is government, the system by which the laws and policy of the state are decided, implemented, and enforced, and the people who play different roles in doing so. Finally there are those we may call the excluded, those who do not hold a strong place in organizations, who have not found collective strength in civil society or representation in government to compensate for, address, or rectify their vulnerability, and who have been exploited as a result. Most people are part of more than one of these groups, many of three, a very few of all four. The company in which the church most often finds itself varies according to the context. This chapter concerns being with the fourth group.

The term "excluded" is broad and unnuanced. As noted earlier in chapter 1, it presupposes a center wherein dwell the sorted and normal, who deign from their benevolence to include those who, for whatever reason, are or become misfits. The excluded are thus those misfits ripe for inclusion, doubtless on the sorted and normal people's terms. What might constitute a more nuanced understanding?

We may think of four broad designations.

1. The **disadvantaged** are those who, collectively, have found themselves unable to access the channels through which the more privileged acquire and secure their social advantage and stability; who have the playing field skewed against them by race, class, or gender; who often live in overcrowded conditions, struggle with inadequate or fragile housing, have little or no access to clean water or sanitary facilities, are in perpetual danger of eviction, and have unsatisfactory clothing and insufficient or less than nutritious food; and who have few or none of the social connections that could provide them a route out or protection against predatory exploiters, adverse weather, or a downturn in health or finances.

2. The **oppressed** are those who have, on account of their race, class, orientation, or other distinguishing characteristic, been deliberately targeted for discrimination, hostility, abuse, or attack; who often find themselves fleeing persecution, living in hiding, practically enslaved, or languishing in jail; and who, as a result, rather than assert their rights and look for opportunities to demonstrate their talents, are more likely to lurk in the shadows, avoid public gaze, and distrust any who seek to walk alongside them.

3. The **afflicted** are those who (as described in *Incarnational Ministry* and illustrated in chapter 6 above), though they are not always economically disadvantaged, find themselves with a highly debilitating long-term or permanent condition

from which there is no envisaged cure or alleviation, and whose survival, let alone well-being, relies on the support and cooperation of neighbors from which it may not be forthcoming, and who are unable to aspire to a conventional life of balanced dependence, interdependence, and independence.

4. The **isolated** are those who, finding themselves in one of or a combination of the preceding plights, or under similar strain, have not been able to find the support or inner resources to avoid mimicking in their own choices and habits the destructive tendencies imposed on them from outside, and have thus become a worse enemy to themselves than any of the candidates lining up externally, with the result that, when circumstances turn against them, there are no comrades or companions left to walk with them or step in to help them, and they find themselves utterly alone and without recourse to resources or refuge.

It's worth pointing out that people can find themselves in more than one category; that the third and fourth categories, and to some extent the second, are not limited by social class; that the more categories you find yourself in, the more challenging your life is likely to be; and that what distinguishes the fourth category from the other three is the tragic distancing of oneself from those who can be and can evoke in oneself the source of life. In my book A *Nazareth Manifesto*, I argued that, while most people assume the human problem is one of limitation, in general, and mortality, in particular, in fact the human predicament is largely one of isolation—and that attempts to overcome limitation often have the effect of increasing isolation. For example, what many people experience as profound loneliness may be exalted by contemporary society as independence or autonomy.

By distinguishing here between the disadvantaged, the oppressed, the afflicted, and the isolated, I want to highlight that the real issue is not material affluence, or even the agency of being able to make choices, but the experience of what I call being with: redemption from the isolation that is humankind's most severe plight. Such isolation is possible—but not inevitable—in the first three of the above conditions as well as being a condition of its own. What the philosophy of being with means in the case of the excluded is to recognize that, while excluded, some might be isolated and some might not; and that mission means primarily seeking to ensure that the excluded are met in their isolation, and thus find resources collectively or individually to make significant changes in their material status, find outlets for their talents, and assert their rights—rather than focus too quickly (in the manner of working for) on "fixing" perceived deficiencies in their material status.

Many treatments of this subject evince anger and dismay at inequality, injustice, indifference, and inertia, often assuming a working-for model of fixing problems and bringing solutions. There is much to be furious about; and inequality, injustice, and inertia are undoubtedly signs of distorted relationships and endemic disorder. But being with assumes that sustainable change comes from people in the context themselves, and that to discover the **glory** one needs to walk alongside them, listen to their perspectives, and refrain from withdrawing to a place of expertise, superiority, or safety. Much anger replicates the shape of exclusion: it takes for granted that the powerful are the center of the story and looks to them to make changes from fear of exposure and bad publicity, enlightened self-interest, benevolent paternalism, or a genuine change of heart. But this underwrites so much of what is awry: being with the excluded means rejecting the assumption that the excluders are the center of the story. It is a practical, visible, and tangible statement that the story is where Jesus is, and Jesus is with the excluded—excluded at birth in a stable, excluded as an infant in Egypt, excluded in obscurity in Nazareth, excluded as a prophet among the rejected of his time, excluded as a criminal, executed in agony and shame.

Being with is about **enjoyment**. It is about entering the lives of the excluded, rather than using perceived economic and social injustice as a stick with which to beat those supposed to be impervious, implicated, or indoctrinated. Elias Chacour, the inimitable Palestinian priest and reconciliation activist, expresses the analysis and challenge of enjoyment succinctly, characteristically attributing its insights to one of his professors.

> If there is a problem somewhere this is what happens. Three people will try to do something concrete to settle the issue. Ten people will give a lecture analyzing what the three are doing. One hundred people will commend or condemn the ten for their lecture. One thousand people will argue about the problem. And one person—only one—will involve themselves so deeply in the true solution that they are too busy to listen to any of it.[1]

The "three" practice what I call working for. The "ten," the "hundred," and the "thousand" employ versions of what I call being for—a category today amplified by the internet and social media. The "one," who is involved deeply and is fully immersed in the context—embodies what I call being with in a spirit of enjoyment. It's not that there isn't a place for the working-for practice of the three—or even the being-for orientation of the ten, the hundred, and the thousand; but in the light of the being-with embodiment of the one,

1. Quoted by Ash Barker, "Epilogue: Challenges and New Possibilities for a New Generation of Mission Workers," in *Living Mission: The Vision and Voices of the New Friars*, ed. Scott A. Bessenecker (Downers Grove, IL: IVP, 2010), 165.

such approaches look like distraction, avoidance, delay, and indulgence. It is as if the only way truly to engage an issue is to renounce the assumption that one will quickly identify, implement, and see the positive results of a "solution." Enjoying means being with even—perhaps especially—when there is no immediate, foreseeable, or even long-term likelihood of a "solution" of this kind, and thus when the other fruits, truths, and depths of the context have time and permission to present themselves.

Thus the encounter of being with begins with **presence** and **participation**. Poverty, discrimination, disadvantage, hunger, homelessness, migrancy: these are not problems to be fixed for a person, they are conditions to be shared with a person, and the sharing with may go a long way to overcome the isolation that in large part constitutes the real issue. Jesus addressed our isolation from God by coming to be with us; the church addresses social isolation by being with those who are alone in their troubles. One can seldom solve someone else's real problem; the best one can usually hope to do is to be alongside others while they find the confidence, motivation, resources, support, and opportunity to address the problem themselves. People are liable to exploitation because they are isolated or alone; when they are accompanied by those who have no desire to take advantage of them, they can find the courage and power to stand up for themselves. The church's response to social disadvantage is often a choice between a being-for approach of advocacy and campaigning and a working-for approach of seeking to solve a person's problems. These apply to the way the church prays as much as to the way the mission of the church is conducted. But transformation comes about most truly from an ethic of being with. Rather than assume it must pray for the oppressed, a congregation might do better to invite one among the oppressed to lead prayers in person and so teach the congregation how things look from the oppressed person's point of view. Thus the church is indeed with God and with the excluded, and it is allowing itself to be changed by those with whom it prays. Then the journey is to recognize that the oppressed are not a "them" that must be encountered but an "us" that needs to be acknowledged and more carefully defined. For a congregation to deny its own oppression or exclude the disadvantaged is to read the passion narrative from the point of view of Pontius Pilate or the trial of Paul from the perspective of Herod Agrippa.

The veteran practitioner of incarnational mission, John Perkins, speaks helpfully of three kinds of incarnation.[2] First there are the remainers. When a formerly homeless person devotes her life to walking with those who continue to be homeless, or when a recovering addict works with those who are still in the grip of drugs, or when people who grew up in what others might call a ghetto choose to remain there and work for good rather than escape and "better" themselves, these are remainers. Jesus was, for most of his earthly life, a remainer. When John says, "He came to what was his own, and his own people did not accept him" (1:11), he is suggesting Jesus never ceased to be a remainer. Remaining is in many ways the ideal form of incarnational mission; but there are two other kinds that supplement and enhance it.

The second strand is that of the relocators. The initiative in this strand lies with people who choose to "move into the neighborhood"—to identify with the disadvantaged, oppressed, afflicted, or isolated by adopting their material conditions and geographical location and living as one of them. Of great significance, of course, is the relocators' motivation

2. See Wayne Gordon and John Perkins, *Making Neighborhoods Whole: A Handbook for Christian Community Development* (Downers Grove, IL: IVP, 2013). See also a helpful account in Craig and Nayhouy Greenfield, "Incarnational: The First Sign," in Bessenecker, ed., *Living Mission*, 36–56.

in doing so: if it is done to "improve" the locality and make it more like the relocators, it is likely to evoke suspicion and hostility from those who are being lived among. If, by contrast, relocators are there out of awareness of their own need, out of humble desire to make relationship, out of longing to meet the God who is most visible in the poor, and with awareness of the pitfalls and power imbalances involved, then things can work out much better. Such purity of heart can be demonstrated by learning the language, adopting cultural practices, withholding judgments until they come with love and understanding, sharing hardships and setbacks, and, in general, walking a mile in local people's shoes. This is what happens when **attention** is added to presence. Jesus was, arguably, a relocator as much as a remainer: as Paul notes, Jesus, "though he was in the form of God, did not regard equality with God as something to be exploited, but emptied himself, taking the form of a slave, being born in human likeness. And being found in human form, he humbled himself and became obedient to the point of death" (Phil. 2:6–8). Jesus lived as a remainer but was born as a relocator.

The third kind of incarnational mission is that of returners. When people leave a place of deprivation, it may be to escape, it may be because their parents or others who seek their flourishing take them elsewhere, it may be because they have an opportunity to develop their talents in another place and take it, it could be because they despise that environment (or their immediate family and neighbors) and can't leave fast enough. The well-known parable that I sometimes call the parable of the two returners is better known as that of the prodigal son; but it's a vivid enough study of why people leave a community—and hardly a deprived one at that. The message is that they cannot be made whole without the humility it takes to return and without the restoration of relationships that only return can make possible. Perhaps the most prominent scriptural returner is Moses: taken away from the Hebrews by basket and Pharaoh's daughter, he returns only to flee again, then he finally returns to become an agent of liberation. The returner models a pattern of being with in perhaps a deeper way than even the remainer or the relocator does (and, eschatologically, Jesus is fundamentally a returner). For, in terms of repentance, all disciples are returners. All repentance is a kind of arriving at the place we started and knowing it for the first time. Being with is always a restoration of something that was once separated, and should not have been.

Attention means avoiding sweeping terms like "poverty" if using them means missing the detail and variety in the dimensions of lived experience. Thus it means distinguishing as I did earlier between the disadvantaged, the oppressed, the afflicted, and the isolated. Each condition has challenges, and they can overlap significantly—but they are not the same. People may be disadvantaged, have poor living conditions, sanitation, job security, and health care, but without any intentional oppression, and with the potential for organizing in their community they may be able to achieve change in their economic and social stability and work with others for a more prosperous future. At the same time they may not define themselves by their deficits but see around them the love of family, the traditions of community, and the joys of a sports team that perhaps take up most or all of their emotional energy. Likewise a person may be oppressed, even to the point of seeking asylum in another country, without being specifically disadvantaged in other ways. But in order to escape oppression in one place, that person may need to accept disadvantage elsewhere. Here is one such story.

My name is Charles. I am a gynecologist from Senegal. I trained in Dakar, Paris and London. I was successful, and I enjoyed a high reputation. But in 2011 my life was threatened because I was helping the LGBT community in Senegal in the area of sexual health. I sought asylum in the UK. I was expecting, as a doctor, to find support, but everything had changed. I had skills to offer: but no one believed me. For 4 years I was dependent on handouts. I slept on buses. I turned up at refugee centres in search of help. As an asylum seeker I was entitled to a card that allowed me £35 of shopping a week. Once I went to the supermarket and the card didn't work. That meant no food for a week. I tried to explain but no one was interested. My life felt worth nothing. I tried to keep myself from losing my mind or killing myself. It seemed even God had forgotten me.

I found a church. Within only a few visits I felt I had a family again. It was a breakthrough for me. God used the people in that church to say "You are part of us—you are our brother." Those people gave me back my dignity.

One day several months later, out walking in the countryside, I came across a sheep in distress. The farmer was anxious because the sheep was bleeding and the vet had been delayed. I quickly realised that it was a breach birth. I went down on my knees and turned the lamb into the right position in the sheep's womb. The lamb was born safely and stood up trembling. Everyone watching clapped. As I was cleaning the blood off my hands someone in the crowd called out, "Are you a vet?" "No," I said. "I am a doctor, but in this country I'm not allowed to work with human beings." The man called back, "We need people like you."

I long to be needed again and to do what God trained me to do. The church gave me back my dignity. I want to use my skills to bring dignity to others. I hope I will be given the chance again.[3]

3. Charles broadcast this story on "Sunday Worship," BBC Radio 4, February 22, 2015.

Again, it's possible to be afflicted and neither disadvantaged nor oppressed (or to be either or both). Here is an account of a person called Jody who meets none of the other three dimensions of what I am calling exclusion (disadvantage, oppression, isolation) and whose poverty is clearly not economic, but whose affliction, though channeled through third-person and first-person-plural expression, is hard to dismiss, deny, or downplay.

Besides Christmas, Mother's Day can be the most difficult day in the calendar for women who aren't mothers, or aren't yet mothers and doubt that they ever will be. Whether you are a couple struggling with infertility, or one of the many women who have been unable to find a suitable partner before your childbearing years draw to a close, or if you haven't had children for one of many other reasons, Mother's Day can be very raw indeed.

Perhaps it would help if we could extend the idea of "mothering" to include all those women who are mothers in their hearts, but aren't biological mothers. To think of "mother" as a verb, not a noun, it's something you do rather than something that you are.

Women without children are 20% of the female population aged 45 and over, but our stories aren't often told, our experience isn't honored and our contribution to the lives of others is often underappreciated. We listen patiently to mothers' delighted talk of their children, and grieve privately that we will never know that joy: first days at school, graduation, perhaps marriage and even grandchildren; a lifetime of photos we will never add to our albums. And yet so often our stoicism in the face of grief is misinterpreted as not really "minding" or perhaps even interpreted as "not liking children."

We non-mothers hide in plain sight, often hungry for

empathy, fielding questions of the most intimate and personal nature which seem to come from all angles. But if you dig a little deeper you'll find that we are those good women around you who make up that "village" it takes to raise a child, to create a community, to sustain a safe and civil society for other people's children to inhabit. And we do so gladly, willingly.

This Mother's Day, let compassion open your heart just a little wider to include all of those who long or longed for motherhood. Although we grieve in private, we are all around you.[4]

Likewise isolation isn't always a result of disadvantage, oppression, or affliction. Here is an account of a person who didn't experience any of these, and yet ended up utterly isolated. His problem wasn't a lack of money or structural class, gender, or racial oppression. He wasn't afflicted by a debilitating long-term or permanent condition. But his situation was nonetheless one of crisis.

My name is Stephen. I work as a housing support officer in Wakefield, West Yorkshire. I am an addict. I took drugs for 23 years. I've been to prison and been homeless many times. My drug-taking started when I lived at home in Scotland at the age of 15. For the next 20 years plus this was my life. It didn't seem a problem to me going to prison; and sometimes being homeless seemed part of the way things were. When I was 37 I lost custody of my 2½-year-old daughter and I realized I had lost control of my life and wanted to make a change.

The problem was that at this lowest point I had no self-

4. Jody broadcast this testimony on "Sunday Worship," BBC Radio 4, March 6, 2016.

227

belief—no confidence in myself, until I met some people who started to believe in me and in who I could be. One support worker managed to get me a flat. But it was the little things I remember most. I moved into that flat late at night so we couldn't get any electricity on till the next day. The support worker remembered I liked to read so she went out and bought me a torch so I could read that night. That simple act of paying attention has stuck in my mind for 8 years and that act of kindness started me on the road to becoming the person I am today.

Once I had stabilized I volunteered for Turning Point. Eventually I gained full-time employment dealing with drugs and alcohol issues. After four years there I moved to the job I have today. I'm now a housing support officer for Wakefield Rent Deposit Scheme, a charity formed 20 years ago through Wakefield Cathedral and Wakefield Council. We feel that the little things we do on a day to day basis like handing out food parcels and vouchers to buy fresh fruit and veg, taking someone to an appointment, or just being there to listen and pay attention to the individual can help to change people's lives for the better. We're trying to support people as they establish themselves in a home after being homeless. Even sending a birthday card can bring a smile and make a difference as someone tries to start again.[5]

I have offered these examples because each one challenges a sweeping notion of poverty or exclusion that lumps together what are in many cases very different kinds of experience and reality. Attention means perceiving these differences and not trying to fit each person into a preexisting notion of exclusion. Jody isn't poor in the conventional sense of disadvantage, and

5. Stephen broadcast this account on "Sunday Worship," BBC Radio 4, December 13, 2015.

her affliction is hard to set alongside quadriplegia or dementia or any such physically or mentally debilitating condition; but her account is undoubtedly one of exclusion, not just from the experience of parenthood but also from the social acceptance that comes with it. Stephen isn't subject to discrimination on any of the conventional grounds; but his life spiraled downwards to the point where he was completely isolated. Charles is a thriving physician at the start of his story, but he becomes disadvantaged through his experience of escaping oppression. There is as much diversity within each of the four dimensions as there is between them. The only thing that can overcome an unhelpful tendency to generalize is the kind of presence that is matched by attention: an attention that twice in his narrative Stephen notes as crucial—first for his redemption, and now for his practice of being with.

Within this attention is an awareness of **mystery**. Poverty is not always and everywhere a bad thing. As a synonym for simplicity and intentional vulnerability to God, neighbor, and creation it has an honored tradition in Christian spirituality and discipleship. Chris Heuertz captures this tension well.

> Poverty in the kingdom of humanity is a lie that dehumanizes the very essence of humanity by marring identity and dignity. Poverty in the kingdom of God releases and enables our identity and dignity to be found in the slain Lamb. Poverty in the kingdom of humanity is offensive. Poverty in the kingdom of God is redemptive. Poverty in the kingdom of humanity is imposed; people who are poor do not choose their poverty, but it is forced upon them. Poverty is embraced in the kingdom of God; Jesus became poor that we might become rich.[6]

6. Christopher L. Heuertz and David Chronic, "Marginal: The Third Sign," in Bessenecker, ed., *Living Mission*, 81.

Being with the excluded means recognizing the power, privilege, and prestige that come with participation in the dominant culture, acknowledging the discipline and deprivation it takes to disengage from continuing to invest all hopes, security, and value in that dominant culture, and yet accepting the extent to which that dominant culture depends on and indeed manufactures and sustains the inequalities and disadvantages that constitute the predominant circumstances of exclusion. Being with the excluded assumes that it is not only appropriate but to a large extent necessary to imitate Jesus and in some respects become poor that others might become rich. Yet it appreciates, as Heuertz makes clear above, that voluntary poverty is not the same as imposed poverty. It is not a solution. It is the entering of a mystery rather than the fixing of a problem.

Delight means finding abundance amid and within (what others might see only as) scarcity. Earlier in this book (chapter 9) I have described how this can be done programmatically through practices such as asset-mapping and appreciative inquiry. Here I simply offer two stories Chris Heuertz tells that beautifully express what this means in the context of being with. He speaks of a returner, Noah, who grew up in Kroo Bay, a slum in Freetown, Sierra Leone, characterized by malnutrition, disease, overcrowding, and flooding, where children outnumber adults by two to one among its population of six thousand. Noah never knew his own mother, and after losing his father at age ten he was brought up by his father's two remaining wives. He returned to his own neighborhood after gaining his education elsewhere. "Noah has entertained the possibility of leaving his home to study finance in England, yet he remains among his friends—the victims of poverty's relentless and oppressive prison." At the bottom of a steep hill is the part of the slum that gets the worst of the flooding and attracts a mountain of human debris and public refuse; here lies a dilapidated church where each week Noah runs the Good News Club for three hundred children. Worship is led by Joseph, a survivor of the 1991–2002 civil war in which he was a child soldier, who sings angelically and leads the children in dance. Noah offers a reflection and then "we watch child after child come forward to have painful boils or open wounds washed and bandaged and gruesome infections treated." Yet delight reigns on the face of Joseph as he praises God for being with him.[7]

Meanwhile, in Romania, a small group of Westerners befriended twenty migrants from Congo. The migrants had been contracted to work long hours in Romania, but after many months without receiving pay their employment was terminated. Originally disadvantaged, they became oppressed. But they were far from isolated: they knew the meaning of delight. In their words, "You need to learn how to worship. We worship until we are drenched in sweat. We worship for hours. In the midst of suffering, hunger and tribulation, we receive strength and encouragement from God through worship."[8] Only through presence, attention, mystery, and participation can one truly perceive delight—which defies the shrewd judgment of the distant observer and finds stores of joy that statistical evaluators and denouncers of structural injustice cannot imagine.

As in a previous chapter (chapter 3) I have left **partnership** till last, because partnership, the dimension most closely identified with working with, is most akin to conventional ways of encountering exclusion and thus most prone to being entered into without the degree of reflection and humility this chapter has been advocating. Questions of exclusion are characterized by the skepticism of genuine change that

7. Heuertz and Chronic, "Marginal: The Third Sign," 87–91.
8. Heuertz and Chronic, "Marginal: The Third Sign," 93.

looks like cynicism, cruelty, or complacency; the emphasis on individual responsibility that looks like judgmental ideology masquerading as self-serving public policy; and the urgency of public intervention that looks like a combination of naïveté, profligacy, and paternalism. In an effort to resist indifference, complacency, and judgmentalism, Christian mission invariably risks naïveté and paternalism. As soon as the flaws of working-for approaches (which often include naïveté and paternalism) are recognized, the reaction can quickly be to assert a new ideology that rejects partnership and assumes there can be no place for any positive agency in relation to exclusion except on the part of the excluded themselves.

I am not making any such assertion. But once again I highlight the importance of attention. There is a difference between disadvantage and oppression. The latter is often in contravention of the law, and so there are cases to be pursued and perpetrators to be brought to account; and, if it is not unlawful, there is often constructive work to be done to ensure that a law is passed of which it is in contravention. This is an obvious role for legislators and advocates and those willing and able to work with survivors of oppression and become architects of a more just legal framework. But disadvantage is not always oppression; it may fall to happenstance or contingency or accident of birth. It is not straightforward, or perhaps even possible, to construct a welfare system that can address every adverse circumstance; and the justice or legislative systems are seldom the best place to go looking for fairness as a birthright. Likewise with affliction, there may be allowances and benefits for those with profound physical needs or mental challenges, and agitating to secure those for some of society's most excluded members is a worthy vocation; but independence and the ability to make one's own choices are not the only or even the most important goals, compared to the capacity to make and sustain fruitful, supportive, and life-giving relationships. And when it comes to isolation, welfare is notoriously seldom the answer; as the case of Stephen narrated above illustrates, what is most required is seldom something that money can buy. The people who made a difference in Stephen's life were those who invested in him beyond the call of their statutory duty.

All of which is an encouragement to recognize that being with in partnership needs to come in the context of presence, attention, and so on—and to emphasize that partnership does not default to matching the excluded person's deficiency and need with the companion's wisdom and skill. Partnership simply means appreciating that when I bring my patience, clumsiness, and network of contacts alongside your gifts, impulsiveness, and relative isolation, you can find a better outcome than you could have done alone, and I can be of more service to you than I could have been by seeking a change in the law or a new governmental policy. Being with does not begin with what Chacour calls "doing something concrete to settle the issue"; and it seldom if ever ends with action, for it is about relationship through and through, as method first but ultimately as goal; but on the way, it may well find deep fulfillment in achieving together what we could seldom even imagine apart.

That word, "together": it's one of the most evocative words in our language. To achieve something alone is satisfying; to reach a goal together is real joy. Any success in life— as athlete, student, company worker—is a team effort. You turn around and see the smiling faces of those who made it possible. There's nothing better. Exclusion is no different. To come out from under the shadow of oppression, to overcome disadvantage, to withstand affliction, to confront whatever got you into such a desolate place—all of this is a team effort. None of us can cope with it alone; but we can face it together.

You can't change people's lives for them; but you can walk alongside them and give them trust, challenge, and encouragement while they find resources and strength to make those changes for themselves. That's the power of the word "together." Alone, there's nothing any of us can do. Together, there's no limit.

Are You Hungry?

At a crucial moment in the film 101 *Dalmatians*, Pongo and Perdita and their fifteen dalmatian puppies are all watching TV, waiting for the right moment to escape from the wicked Cruella De Vil. One of the puppies, Rolly, despite being captivated by the film, says, "I'm hungry, Mother. I'm hungry." Perdita, "Now Rolly, you've just had your dinner." Rolly insists, "But I *am*, just the same. I'm so hungry I could eat a...a whole elephant."

There's two kinds of hunger. There's a hunger that has a name. It's a hunger where you know what you want but you haven't got it or can't have it: when you interviewed for a job, and you can't understand why they didn't appoint you; when you long with all your heart to have a baby, but it's not happening; where you're dying for something to eat, but the cupboard's bare; when you just want something, something in your life to go right for a change, but people keep letting you down. Such hunger can become all-consuming, transforming your temper, your relationships, your patience, your clarity of thought, your whole character. We are what we eat, they

---

A sermon preached at St. Martin-in-the-Fields on February 28, 2016.

235

say; we're also capable of becoming contorted into the shape of what we hunger for.

But there's another kind of hunger. It's a hunger that lingers deep, disturbingly, in the bottom of your soul, but it doesn't have a name. There's no simple solution to it, no hot meal or job title or box ticket that will satisfy it. The Irish band U2 famously articulated this second kind of hunger when they sang with longing and bewilderment, "I have climbed the highest mountains, I have run through the fields Only to be with you; I have run I have crawled I have scaled these city walls Only to be with you: But I still haven't found What I'm looking for." Rather more vividly the Rolling Stones, tired of the ordinary and weary of the wild, sang, "I can't get no satisfaction, 'Cause I try and I try and I try and I try...." The reason these songs stay in the memory decades after their release is that they identify a point deep in the gut where hunger lingers, the hunger that doesn't have a name, the restless, yearning, aching, gnawing, longing hunger that knows when it hasn't found what it's looking for, that knows when it's got no satisfaction.

The psychologist Abraham Maslow believed he could find a causal connection between these two kinds of hunger. In 1943 he published a paper explaining what he called the hierarchy of human needs. He made the point that we can't really engage with higher matters until our basic physiological needs are met. Above our physiological needs are our safety needs, and above those are our belonging needs; next come our esteem needs. Finally we get to this wonderful point where we can work on our self-actualization. (I hope you don't mind, but I'd be grateful if we could all keep working for the next few years on my esteem needs and then I'll let you know when I'm about ready to work on my self-actualization.) The trouble is, even if we've never experienced near-starvation, we can all more or less express vividly what the first kind of hunger feels like—and what it's like to devour a meal when you've been waiting hours and feeling faint and beginning to shake with longing for food. But the second kind of hunger—that's more difficult. How do you describe what it feels like to realize you still haven't found what you're looking for?

Isaiah chapter 55 is precisely about these two kinds of hunger and the difference between them. For fifty years in Babylonian exile, Israel was focused on the first kind of hunger—quite simply, "I want to go home." Everything that was wrong was crystalized in one simple fact—Israel was a thousand miles from the Promised Land, and on any hierarchy of needs returning to the land of David and Solomon was foundational. But Isaiah chapter 55 marks a transition into the second kind of hunger. Because Israel did go home from Babylon. Israel did return to the Promised Land. Jerusalem was restored, the Temple rebuilt, the walls raised again. But when all that was done, Israel was still hungry. "I'm hungry, Mother. I'm hungry." "Now Israel, you've just had your dinner." "But I *am*, just the same. I'm so hungry I could eat a … a whole elephant." It turned out going home wasn't all that Israel was hungry for.

"Why do you spend your money for that which is not bread, and your labour for that which does not satisfy?" These are the resonant words of Isaiah to Israel. It's a question that points out the difference between the hunger that has a name and the hunger that doesn't have a name. Working out the difference between the two is the key to ministry and mission.

The 2004 film *The Chorus* is set in southeast France in 1949. A tyrannical headmaster, Monsieur Rachin, presides over a reform school for out-of-control boys, set in an old castle known as Fond de l'Étang (which translates as "Bottom of the Pond" or "Rock Bottom"). An out-of-work music teacher, Clément Mathieu, arrives to replace a teacher who's leaving because his arm has been savaged by a pupil. The headmaster's regime is simple: he seeks control through fear, and he gives the boys enough food to keep them healthy and strict discipline to keep them compliant. The new teacher Monsieur Mathieu faces a high level of hostility and studied aggravation, and his more lenient policy on punishment brings him into conflict with the censorious headmaster.

But the story really begins when Monsieur Mathieu decides to teach the children to sing. All but one has some kind of serviceable voice, and most of the boys play along because it's less demanding than the regular curriculum. The one boy, Pierre, who keeps aloof, is the wildest of them all; when his mother, out of her depth and unmarried, visits, Monsieur Mathieu lies to her and says Pierre is at the dentist when in fact he's being punished. This wins Pierre's trust, and Monsieur Mathieu begins to realize that the wild and suspicious Pierre has an astounding treble voice. Gradually, despite the headmaster's increasing anxiety and envy, the chorus of boys grows in skill and confidence, performing for the local countess. But it cannot last. Part of the school burns down due to arson, Monsieur Mathieu is held responsible and fired, and he's forced to leave without saying goodbye. But then you see two men, fifty years later, leafing through the scrapbook Monsieur Mathieu wrote up about his time at Fond de l'Étang. And you remember the film started with a sixty-two-year-old orchestral conductor at the height of his powers performing a Strauss waltz. And you realize this is that same man, and that same man is called Pierre, and he was the tearaway delinquent who became the treble soloist and is now the living embodiment that Monsieur Mathieu's work was not in vain, but brought forth a hundredfold.

The film is about the same distinction between the hunger that has a name and the hunger that has no name. The boys know all about the first kind of hunger. They want food, they want some control over their lives, they want exercise, they want to make misery for anyone who tries to pin them down. But the real drama of the story is about the second kind of hunger. The boys are very, very angry. But most of them aren't exactly sure what they're angry about or whom they're angry with. They're hungry, but food and exercise go little or no distance to meeting their hunger.

And this is the crucial point. On the surface *The Chorus* is another inspiring-teacher story, like *Dead Poets Society* or, for those who go back to 1967 and Sidney Poitier, *To Sir, with Love*. But the crucial point is that Monsieur Mathieu doesn't give the boys what they think they want. He doesn't meet the first kind of hunger in any significant way. He takes a huge gamble on reaching them in the hunger that they don't have a name for. And that's where the film becomes more than a heart-warming story and turns into an important analogy for Christian mission.

We often think of practical Christianity as striving to meet people's hunger, the hunger that has a name: for the starving, food; for the thirsty, water; for the naked, clothing; for the sick, medicine. All of which is good and right and true. But like U2 and the Rolling Stones, people want and need more than that. Almost always, what they want is something no one can give them. If they assume someone can give it to them, they generally leave behind them a trail of wreckage of those from or in whom they've failed to find the answer to their hunger. Christianity isn't simply about satisfying people's hunger. It's a huge gamble on the hunch that what people are really hungry for is something they don't know the name of, and wouldn't initially recognize even when they found it.

And what is that mysterious discovery, that extraordinary food? It's the wondrous truth that there's something even deeper, even more long-lasting, and even more insatiable than our hunger. And that's God's hunger for us. "For as the heavens are higher than the earth, so are my ways higher than your ways and my thoughts than your thoughts," we're told in Isaiah chapter 55. God's hunger is greater than ours. But God knows what that hunger is for. It's for us. And discovering that is for us like discovering choral music was for the boys in that reform school. For some of us, like Pierre, it unearths a gift that was longing to get out. For others, it's a realization that together we can make something beautiful we could never make alone, that there's a place for all shapes and sizes and voices and energies in a song that takes all our energies to make but comes from a force much bigger than us. Bigger than a whole elephant.

Are you hungry? Does your hunger have a name, like a yearning for a job or a partner or a home or a new start? Or is your hunger deeper and more insatiable than that, something that even gaining those precious things won't assuage? "Listen carefully to me," says Monsieur Mathieu, says Isaiah, "and eat what is good, and delight yourselves in rich food." "Come, buy wine and milk without money and without price." It's free but not cheap—it's priceless but for everybody. If you're hungry—deeply, deeply hungry—hear the good news, the news that you've been waiting all this time for: God's hungry. Hungry for you.

Index of Names and Subjects

Delight, 14–15; and being with the excluded, 230–31; and being with government, 205–9; and being with the hostile, 107; and being with institutions, 181–82; and being with the lapsed, 36–40; and being with organizations, 150–54; and being with seekers, 48–49; and being with those of no professed faith, 73–74; and being with those of other faiths, 95

De Officiis (Cicero), 166

Discipleship/disciples, 16, 17–18, 61, 148; and ministry, 16

Doctor, DePayne Middleton, 116

Donne, John, 155

Dostoyevsky, Fyodor, 33–34

Duke University: chaplaincy at, 171–89 *passim*; motto of (*Eruditio et Religio*), 179; transformation of from a provincial college into a national university, 175–76; the undergraduate classroom as the heart of the university, 176–77; unique geographical and cultural position of, 179; and the university's hospital and basketball team, 181

Education: the Harvard faculty's description of the aims of, 168; influence of Augus-

tine on, 143; renaissance humanism's view of, 168

Eliot, George, 32–33

Enemies, Jesus's seven categories of, 103

Enjoyment, 15; and being with the excluded, 220–21; and being with government, 213–14; and being with the hostile, 108; and being with institutions, 185–86; and being with the lapsed, 36–40; and being with neighbors, 125–26; and being with organizations, 150–54; and being with seekers, 55–56; and being with those of no professed faith, 70–71; and being with those of other faiths, 92–93

Entrust, 167–68, 167n3

Equal Justice Initiative, 124

Erdozain, Dominic, 31–33

Ethiopian eunuch, the, 54

Evangelism, 49; cold-calling evangelism, 74; as a means toward the end of being with, 76

Excluded, the, 22, 216–34 *passim*; the afflicted, 217–18, 226–27, 232–33; and anger, 219; and attention, 223–29; and delight, 230–31; the disadvantaged, 217, 224, 232; and enjoyment, 220–21; and glory, 219; the isolated, 218, 219, 227–28, 233; and mystery, 229–30; the oppressed, 217, 224–25, 232; and participa-

Index of Scripture References